The Essence of
VEDANTA

The Essence of
VEDANTA
BRIAN HODGKINSON

CHARTWELL
BOOKS, INC.

This edition printed in 2006 by
CHARTWELL BOOKS, INC.
A Division of **BOOK SALES, INC.**
114 Northfield Avenue
Edison, New Jersey 08837

ISBN-13: 978-0-7858-2116-8
ISBN-10: 0-7858-2116-3

Printed in China

Cover illustration: Sunset on the Yamuna River, Agra, India
(courtesy Corbis).

To my wife, Catherine

Contents

Acknowledgments

Many people over many years have contributed to the making of this book, but I wish to thank, especially, Michael Shepherd for several valuable comments, Dr Stephen Thompson for the benefit of his extensive knowledge of Sanskrit, Tessa Rose of Arcturus for her constant support, Matthew Cory for some stimulating editing, my son David and daughter-in-law Catherine for advice in several areas, and my wife for her unfailing patience. None of the above are responsible for its shortcomings.

Every effort has been made to contact the copyright holders of material quoted in this book and seek their permission for its inclusion. We thank the following for their kindness in granting permissions: Advaita Ashrama; Cambridge University Press; Munshiram Manoharlal; Oxford University Press, India; Oxford University Press, New York; Shanti Sadan; Sri Ramanasramam; The Study Society; Watkins Books.

Any oversights are sincerely regretted, and if drawn to the attention of the publisher will be rectified at the earliest opportunity.

Introduction

When I was about seventeen I heard a radio talk by Peter Strawson, an eminent Oxford philosopher, about free will. It was fascinating. He discussed questions such as whether we experience anything called freedom of the will, when we deliberately raise an arm. My interest in such matters has never faltered, but the direction of my investigations into them has undergone a sea change. After three years enjoying the delights and trials of studying at Oxford, at a time when it was regarded as the world centre of modern analytical or linguistic philosophy, and another five years teaching the subject to bemused undergraduates at Sussex University, by the greatest good fortune I came across a wholly different approach to the subject in the form of Vedanta.

Philosophy did not cease for me to be an intellectual enquiry into the fundamental aspects of human existence, but it became, in addition, a matter of learning how to live in accordance with the principles that Vedanta revealed. Above all, it showed how my view of myself had been mistaken. No longer could I believe that in my innermost self I was a separate individual. Life continued much as before, in so far as I had a career, got married, had a son, and enjoyed the benefits of living in England, where individual freedom happily remains paramount. (There was no paradox about individualism in this.) But my view of the world was slowly transformed the more I learnt of Vedanta. Other people were no longer separated from me, as beings with an existence exclusively their own. At heart we were one, even if from day to day we seemed to become occasionally angry, envious, bored or shy with one another. However much these feelings intervened, there was always recourse to the one sure principle of Vedanta, that all are *Brahman*, the universal spirit.

Similarly, my relationship with the natural world lost a sense of alienation, prevalent since adolescence. The beauty of natural things – animals, trees, flowers, the sea and mountains – had always been acutely felt, but it had been something I wanted in vain to grasp for myself. Like Wordsworth, I believed that 'there hath past away a glory from the earth'. Henceforth, that beauty became an aspect of the beauty of oneself, not the self of me as an individual, but the self that shines in the hearts of all.

Vedanta hinges upon this truly remarkable idea, that everything, without any exception whatsoever, is the one spirit. Indeed, if one could fully appreciate and remember this from moment to moment, so that it became the way in which one lived, rather than a thought, there would be little need to learn more of the whole vast system of ideas that Vedanta has become over millennia. For all the rest is ultimately no more than an introduction to, or preparation for, the recognition of unity, the oneness of spirit.

Vedanta is a philosophical system associated especially with India. Its greatest teachers, its key texts and by far the majority of its students or followers have all been Indian. To approach it, however, as a specifically Indian system, would be entirely misleading. For, above all, Vedanta is universal. What else could it be, when its central questions are those of all mankind? What am I? What is the universe? What is my relationship to it? Most thinking men and women throughout history have, at some time in their lives, asked – perhaps felt – such questions, and every nation has brought forth some who have been driven by similar enquiries into deep realms of thought or emotion.

One might argue that even the word 'philosophy' is inappropriate in relation to Vedanta, for philosophy means the love of wisdom, and Vedanta perhaps might be better described as wisdom itself. For, as Socrates claimed in the *Symposium*, love is really no more than an intermediary, a halfway house on the way to the union of the lover with the beloved. To claim, however, an identity between Vedanta and wisdom is a dangerous idea. As a system that can be studied from the words of master teachers and from ancient texts, it is no more than a guide that may point in the direction of the truth. Wisdom, on the other hand, is practical. The wise live what they know. They practise it in their lives. No words, spoken or written, can do this on behalf of anyone. Hence Vedanta as a system is a kind of manual of wisdom, not wisdom itself.

The analogy can be pursued further. If you want to learn to drive, you go to a driving school. If the school just sold you a driving manual, you would feel seriously short-changed. Likewise, the practical nature of Vedanta – as wisdom – can perhaps only be learnt from a guru, a teacher who has himself acquired wisdom from study and practice at the feet of his own master. What use then is a manual? Why read a book on driving or a book on Vedanta? There are several answers to this question. Trivially, one may simply want to know something of how other people drive or live their lives. More importantly, the manual may supplement or reinforce the knowledge derived from a teacher. Or it may act as a substitute, albeit a poor one, when no teacher is available. One could, if it were absolutely necessary, learn to drive a car just from a manual. Since in the Western world there are few genuine teachers of Vedanta, even a book on Vedanta may go some way towards enabling a willing student to practise its principles, if only by pointing him or her towards texts such as the Upanishads.

What then is the vital difference between what might be called theory and practice? Let us take another specific principle of Vedanta – the astonishing statement 'I do nothing at all.' Even in theory this may sound strange. What it means is that everything is done by the body, senses and mind as instruments. The self – I – does nothing. It merely observes, for observation is not itself an act. What then can this mean in practice? One may accept the principle in theory, but still firmly believe that one is, in fact, walking or driving a car. When the wise walk or drive, however, they do so in the certain knowledge that everything is done, even an emergency stop, by mind, senses and body alone. They are not identified with the act. No verbal instruction could bring a student to such a point of wisdom, though it may prepare the way.

In relation to religion, Vedanta forms indeed the philosophical basis of Hinduism, but just as students of Plato may recognize the master's teaching in St John's gospel without necessarily being Christians, so too students of Vedanta have no need whatsoever to embrace the chief religion of India. As a medieval historian once said of Chartres Cathedral, it is best appreciated as a spiritual, rather than as a religious, building. Vedanta also is about the spirit – the one universal spirit – but it is not about religion. People of every religion, and of none, may all drink from the waters of its spiritual depths.

This book begins by discussing briefly the historical and literary origins of Vedanta, and by outlining the work of Sankara, the early medieval master of the dominant form of Vedanta, known as *Advaita* (non-dualism) (*see* Ch. 1). It continues with the major subject of knowledge (*see* Ch. 2). As our predominantly scientific age is reluctantly beginning to accept, knowledge is by no means limited to the field of empirical enquiry. Even in matters which can be settled empirically – the colour of the sky or the mass of an atom – who is the knower? The Sanskrit word for knowledge (*jnana*) has connotations of knowing both the object of knowledge and the subject – in other words, of a unity of knowledge rarely considered in Western thought. Obviously such a concept raises problems, like how can the knower be known, but Vedanta proposes subtle responses to such analytical questions.

The topic of the self is introduced early on (*see* Ch. 3), for it is the key to understanding all else. The individual self is found wanting. Its very existence is undermined by many observations and arguments, not unlike some used by modern Western philosophers from Hume to Wittgenstein. For example, what qualities can be attributed to the self which are not, in fact, qualities of a body or mind? So if the self has no qualities, how can it be distinguished from other putative selves? Vedanta's resolution of this 'annihilation' of the self is the simple conclusion that the self is indeed one, that there are no other selves: 'I am *Brahman*' or 'This *Atman* (individual self) is *Brahman*'. Thus the notion of *Advaita,* or non-duality, becomes the cornerstone.

By an obvious progression the concept of consciousness follows (*see* Ch. 4). For what is the self, if not consciousness? Everyone can easily identify with such an idea – that in themselves, beyond body and mind, lies a conscious self. In practice, of course, we often identify ourselves with the body, and especially with the mind. We assume that 'I am thinking, doubting, imagining and so on'; but on reflection we know that we are consciousness, rather than these thoughts, doubts and the rest. Vedanta, however, is concerned to uproot the idea that each of us is a separate unit of consciousness, a kind of conscious blob, sharing the experience of lumps of matter with other conscious blobs called animate creatures. It does this by breaking down the concept of an individual consciousness and replacing it with universal consciousness. Here the analogy of space, which similarly may seem to have discrete parts but in reality is one, is a favourite device. But so too are arguments that assert the omnipresence of consciousness throughout the three states of waking, dreaming and sleeping. These states themselves appear to be individual, but the *Mandukya* Upanishad makes it clear that they are not.

Why do we need to learn all this? Is it merely out of intellectual curiosity? The next topic (*see* Ch. 5) replies in one word – liberation. Few people can say truthfully that they believe themselves to be completely free. If we are lucky, we may live in a relatively free country, such as Britain or the United States, under the rule of law, with a democratically elected government and a free press – but that is essentially an outer freedom, or freedom from arbitrary external restraints. What of inner freedom, the absence of stress, fear, suffering, anxiety or neurosis? Vedanta goes further still. It offers freedom from all limitations, even those seemingly imposed by the very fact of having a body and mind. For freedom, or liberation, is the complete and final realization that one is the pure self, untouched by any trace of bodily or mental inhibitions. It is achieved entirely by the removal of all limitations or impediments (*upadhis*), such as the belief that 'I am this body'.

We then move to an examination of Vedanta's appraisal of nature (*see* Ch. 6). Once more we find a highly comprehensive concept (*prakriti*), for it is not limited to what Westerners might call the natural world, but includes all animate and inanimate objects – material things, living creatures, humanity as physical organisms and minds, and also the space and time that are the matrix of all these. It excludes only the self or *Brahman*. How then can the principle of *Advaita* be retained, if self and nature are distinguished from each other? At this point we meet a crux. The solution is the introduction of the concept of *maya*, perhaps the most difficult aspect of the Vedanta system. *Maya* is the dream of *Brahman*, the grand illusion of the world, which contains all that we ordinarily believe to exist. For all of that is, in fact, an illusion; it has no independent reality. In so far as it exists, it does so as a manifestation of *Brahman* itself. In other words, the world that we experience (*prakriti* or nature) is *Brahman* seen through human perception, the means of which – sense organs and the mind – are themselves all part of the illusion.

Such an account inevitably raises questions about time, since time itself is no more than a chief feature of this illusion (*see* Ch. 7). *Brahman* manifests in time past, time present and time future, but under the form of cycles of great ages, which repeat in regular succession, each exhibiting dominant types of humanity. In contrast to Darwinism, Man is seen as declining in power and intelligence throughout each cycle, but reappearing in pristine shape at the beginning of each. Moreover, individual men and women live, not one life, but very many, incurring in each life an accumulation of effects determined by how well or badly they have lived. This heritage from earlier lives (*sanskara*) sets the pattern for each life, leaving only the path of knowledge as the way of escape from unending recurrence.

There follows an account of the Vedantic philosophy of mind (*see* Ch. 8), which looks at several issues raised earlier. Are there many minds or one only? Does mind have discernible parts or functions? Can it be controlled? Is there a mind/body problem? Vedanta's analysis of mind is rewardingly simple. The principal functions of mind are explicitly stated, and shown to constitute the link between consciousness, on one hand, and the senses and body, on the other. Once again we are reminded that, in reality, mind also is no more than an aspect of self, a kind of apparent focus of the light of consciousness that pervades all.

Despite its emphasis on unity, Vedanta has been interpreted in various ways (*see* Ch. 9). The most radical and most rigorous form is that of *Advaita* or non-dualism, which is primarily the substance of this book. Yet there are two other principal systems credited with the term Vedanta, but entertaining some degree of dualism. The first, theism, stems mainly from the medieval teacher, Ramanuja, who believed that devotion (*bhakti*) was the chief means to liberation, and that in reality Man and God are not both the one *Brahman*. God is *Brahman*, the eternal spirit, and Man fulfils himself absolutely by reaching a state permanently in the presence of God. The second system, that of Madhva, goes further, asserting an outright dualism between God and animate creatures, the latter retaining features of their individual identity, even when finally attaining to the direct contemplation of God. Whereas Ramanuja taught that Man has no existence independent of God, Madhva's view was that animate creatures are ontologically distinct from God, and hence can suffer eternal damnation in separation from Him.

Another form of Vedanta, which complements, rather than contrasts, with *Advaita* Vedanta is that of Word-*Brahman* (*Shabda Brahman*) (*see* Ch. 10).This identifies *Brahman* with the word *OM*, and views the world as the development of this primal sound through the multitude of names that correspond to the 'objects' denoted by them. These names are not the words found in vernacular languages, or even in Sanskrit, but are seen as word sounds of an underlying natural language. Word-*Brahman* is consistent with the Vedantic principle that all manifestation is name and form only, as an aspect of the illusion of *maya*. Grammar, the study of the laws by which words and sentences are constructed from their rudimentary forms, also becomes a major area of study, which is briefly examined.

Finally, social issues in the philosophy of Vedanta are discussed (*see* Ch. 11). Here the basic concept is that of law (*dharma*), which ranges over legal or prescriptive rules, morality and laws of nature as understood in the natural sciences, like physics. *Dharma* is the will of *Brahman*, and hence is inexorable, which once more raises questions about Man's role in the universe and his free will. Last, but not least in its significance for the Western world, Vedanta puts forward a controversial view of class and caste. Modern India is often seen as a country struggling to escape from an outmoded and unjust caste system. The distinction between class and caste, however, suggests that Indian society was originally founded on a just system of classes, the proper meaning of which has been forgotten. Indeed, the West could learn much about social justice from an examination of class and law as stated in the tradition of Vedanta.

Such a conclusion can be generalized. The Western world currently exhibits untold confusion in the realm of thought concerning fundamental issues. As John Donne wrote:

> 'And new philosophy calls all in doubt,
> The element of fire is quite put out;
> The sun is lost, and th'earth, and no man's wit
> Can well direct him, where to look for it.'
> *(An Anatomy of the World: The First Anniversary)*

In our time, Vedanta is where to look for it. The Sun is our source of light. What we require today is the light of knowledge, and it is to the ancient wisdom of Vedanta that we may turn for the knowledge that underlies the study, not only of law and society, but of all matters that concern mankind. Above all, one may find there the deepest insight into oneself.

Chapter 1

Origins

The Veda

About a thousand years before the earliest Greek philosophers of whom we have record, a collection of Sanskrit writings known as the Veda, which means knowledge, were made in India. Their authorship is unknown, which is in keeping with the traditional claim that the Veda were originally 'heard' by sages and then passed on orally through generations of teachers. They were finally written down to ensure their preservation. The Veda, indeed, are said to be coeval with mankind – with the creation of humanity came the simultaneous creation of the knowledge required to live as a conscious being in the universe. Hence they are seen as a record of natural law in its widest sense. It is not surprising, therefore, that the system of Vedanta derived from the Veda is probably the most comprehensive exposition of philosophy found at any time in the world.

The first Veda, the Rig Veda (which may possibly date back to about 4000 BC), contains mainly prayers in praise of gods associated with the elements, such as fire and air, and in supplication for health, offspring, cattle and so on, in addition to rules concerning the ceremonies and sacrifices when prayers were offered. The later Yagur Veda and Sama Veda borrowed much from the Rig Veda, and were largely for the use of priests. Finally, the fourth Veda, the Atharva Veda, contained original hymns and incantations of a more popular nature, intended, for example, to cure illness. By tradition, Vyasa, the legendary author of the great epic, the *Mahabharata*, was the compiler of the Veda in the form in which they have come down to us. Since, however, his name means in Sanskrit 'compiler, arranger or divider', it is by no means certain that one man was responsible for both works.

The 'triple canon' of Vedanta

Such material, unpromising as it may appear to the modern mind and associated with an age when sacrifice was a central concept, gave rise to the deeply philosophic Upanishads. These were intended to make more explicit the hidden teachings of the Veda, even though they themselves remain often mystical in content and style. Probably written in the early part of the first millennium BC, the Upanishads are less concerned with ritual. The earliest ones, such as the *Chandogya* and the *Brihadaranyaka*, are highly speculative, whilst the later, such as the *Svetasvatara*, are more devotional. Usually they proceed by rational discussion, using dialogue and stories enlivened with poetic language – the later ones are written in metre – with the aim of examining the most fundamental questions of existence, reality, nature and freedom. Over one hundred Upanishads are extant. An example of a verse gives a clue to their style:

> 'In the beginning this was but the absolute Self alone. There was nothing else whatsoever that winked. He thought, "Let me create the worlds."'
>
> (*Aitareya* Upanishad, I i I, in *The Eight Upanishads*, Vol. 2, p. 20)

Upanishad means 'sitting at the feet' (of a master). Such a meaning emphasizes the vital idea inherent in Indian philosophy that truth is generally discovered by questions asked by a pupil of his or her master or guru. This oral tradition, which goes so far as to exclude the possibility of knowledge arising from the mere reading of books, is expressed in the *Taittiriya* Upanishad by describing the teacher on one side, the pupil on the other, discourse joining them, and knowledge arising between. However, an alternative version of the word Upanishad gives it the discursive meaning 'setting at rest ignorance by revealing the knowledge of the supreme spirit'. A pithier statement of the whole intention of Vedanta could hardly be found.

In addition to the Upanishads, Vedanta, which means 'the end or conclusion of the Veda', recognizes two other major works as being especially authoritative, namely the *Brahma Sutras* and the *Bhagavad Gita*. The first is attributed to Badarayana, a philosopher of the early centuries AD, though tradition identifies him with Vyasa. *Sutras*, literally 'threads', are potent aphorisms stating the essential points of a topic. For example, a *sutra* of three Sanskrit words says, 'from which – birth, etc. – of this', which actually means '(That is Brahman) from which (are derived) the birth, etc. (of this universe)'. The missing words are established from the context by commentators. Such extraordinary conciseness – a feature of other Sanskrit writers, like the great grammarian, Panini – owes its effect to the fact that the *Brahma Sutras* are a systematic explanation of the leading concepts in the Upanishads. Not surprisingly, over the centuries the Upanishads have acquired learned commentators, the greatest of whom is the 8th-century AD philosopher, Sankara, whose *Brahma Sutra Bhasya* (commentary) itself became an authoritative statement of Vedanta.

Third in the 'triple canon' of Vedanta is the *Bhagavad Gita*, undoubtedly the best loved and most widely read of the sacred books of India. Since it forms a part of the *Mahabharata*, its authorship has been assigned also to Vyasa. It relates a conversation between the great warrior, Arjuna, and his charioteer, Krishna, who in reality is the Lord of All, or the universal spirit. Arjuna despairs at the prospect of a fight to the death with the family of the Kauravas, blood relatives of his own Pandava family. Krishna recalls him to his duty as a member of the warrior class (*kshatriya*). By a series of philosophical arguments he wins Arjuna over to the cause of fighting in a just war without regard for the imagined consequences. Even the death of his honoured friends and relatives is as nothing beside the fulfilment of his role in the service of the one true self (*Atman*), which alone is real:

> 'Who thinks the Self may kill, who thinks the Self
> Itself be killed, has missed the mark of truth.
> Self is not born, nor does it ever die;
> It does not come to life, not having been,
> Nor, having been, does it thereafter cease.
> Eternal, ancient, ever-present Self,
> Though bodies are cut down, lives on intact.'
> (*Bhagavad Gita*, II, 19–20, p. 47)

The popularity of the *Gita* stems not only from its brilliant use of imagery and metre, but also from its appeal as a story, familiar to all, of a man borne down by the weight of emotional suffering and moral dilemma. Krishna's words offer hope and salvation to all in a like condition of mind on the battlefield, or in other painful yet more humdrum circumstances. The appeal is to the heart as well as to the mind; as much to those who look for some way of devotion, as to those who seek intellectual satisfaction. Even to those who can do little but work, Krishna offers the way of action, which opens the path to knowledge, if it is followed without desire for the results of work.

Sankara

Sankara also played a part in clarifying the Vedantic content with regard to the *Bhagavad Gita*. His commentary on the *Gita* draws out the philosophical concepts and arguments to reveal a system of ideas fundamentally the same as those of the major Upanishads and the *Brahma Sutras*. Likewise, he wrote lengthy commentaries on the Upanishads themselves, so that when combined with his own treatises and sacred poetry, his work as a commentator on the scriptures has made him by general assent the greatest single exponent of Vedanta philosophy. Like Plato, whose influence on Western philosophy is perhaps comparable to Sankara's on that of India, he often used a dialectical method of assertion and counter-assertion. Unlike Plato, however, whose putative opponents often raise minor objections or merely nod agreement, Sankara's 'opponent' is sometimes acutely analytic or is representative of a whole school of opposing thought. This heightens the intensity of the debate about major issues, such as the ontology of matter and spirit and the relationship between the individual self (*Atman*) and the universal self (*Brahman*).

Sankara is thought to have died at the age of thirty-two. Yet not only did he write voluminously; he also travelled extensively from his home in south India in order to debate with opponents, both Vedantists and those of other faiths and philosophical persuasions. At that time Indian philosophy and religion were in a state of turmoil, with Buddhism making large inroads into the previously prevalent Hinduism, and with unorthodox forms of Vedanta also widespread. By dialectical skill and depth of thought Sankara refuted his opponents and enabled traditional Vedanta to re-assert itself. His aim was always to purify the teaching of the scriptures, and to restore the true meaning of Vedanta. To this end he also set up a seat of orthodox Vedanta in each quarter of India, and Sankaracharyas (*acharya* = teacher) still teach at these centres, which contain *ashrams* (monastic communities) for students and disciples. Visitors, including Western followers of Vedanta, have been welcomed at these centres.

Advaita Vedanta

What then is this traditional Vedanta, from which other Vedantic teachings deviate, and which confronts other philosophical systems even within India, such as Buddhism and Jainism? Sankara taught the doctrine of *Advaita* (non-duality). In the West, duality in philosophy has been associated mainly since the time of Descartes with the mind/body problem. Descartes thought he had established that mind and body were two distinct substances, one immaterial, one made of matter; the former the subject or perceiver of things and events in the material world and itself consisting of thought, doubt, feeling and similar subjective states. Subsequent Western philosophers have often taken this dichotomy as a starting point, though in the 20th century some have argued that Ryle, Wittgenstein and others have laid to rest Descartes' 'ghost in the machine'.

However, Sankara's non-duality is more far reaching. It argues against the yet more fundamental duality of self and the world. Very few Western philosophers have been so bold as to deny the obvious distinction between a self that perceives, thinks, feels and acts and an objective world of things, whether bodily, mental or whatever. Clearly this non-duality in some sense identifies the self with the world. From a Western standpoint such an identity is usually classed as pantheism. Yet Sankara is not a pantheist. In *Advaita* the self is not equated with the world, nor merely immanent in it. It is both immanent and transcendent, both in the world and beyond it. To explain how this is possible made great demands even on the acute mind of Sankara.

Other orthodox systems

Sankara himself never claimed originality; nor do any orthodox Vedantists. His view was that the doctrine of *Advaita* is intrinsic to the Upanishads, the *Brahma Sutras* and the *Bhagavad Gita*. However, other interpretations of these scriptures are possible. Vedanta contains schools of thought which do not go so far as Sankara's *Advaita*. The 12th- to 13th-century AD teachers, Ramanuja and Madhva, for example, argued for a dualistic theism and an outright dualism respectively, yet they held to such orthodox beliefs as transmigration of the individual self, and *Brahman* as the material cause of the world. Further systems have evolved from the ultimate source of the Vedas, but are not regarded as within the field of Vedanta as such, although they are considered orthodox. These are *Nyaya*, *Vaisesika*, *Samkhya*, *Yoga* and *Mimamsa*, and they depart from Vedanta into the fields of logic, atomism, atheism, austerities and semantics, even though on some issues they are not opposed to it. Unorthodox systems of Indian philosophy, notably Buddhism and Jainism, are too far from Vedanta to bear much comparison.

The importance of language

One other aspect of the Vedanta system needs a brief introduction. Philosophy always leads into questions regarding language, since it is expressed in language, and since the relationship between what exists and the words used to refer to what exists demands elucidation. With its study of picture theories of meaning, linguistic analysis and so on, 20th-century Western philosophy amply bears this out. Vedanta is no exception. It contains a whole approach to philosophical problems from the standpoint of language, using concepts such as '*sphota*', a kind of explosion of consciousness associated with meaning. Most significantly, perhaps, by regarding Sanskrit as the purest and most seminal of existing languages, Vedanta investigates central concepts through a study of their derivation from verbal roots (*dhatus*) and the explanations given by traditional grammarians, notably the great Panini of the 4th century BC. Once more we find the underlying principle that the most profound knowledge is not drawn from empirical experience and human thought, as Western philosophers particularly since the Florentine Renaissance would claim, but rather that it lays open (or perhaps hidden!) for discovery in recorded teachings handed down from time immemorial.

The story of the mahout

Finally, as a leaven in the weight of learning, the teachers of Vedanta have related many customary stories or legends, some of which can be traced back to such ancient literature as the *Puranas*, collections of myths and legends, of which the most popular deal with the early life of the divine incarnation, Krishna. They usually give point to philosophical doctrine with a practical case, much like the stories of Zen Buddhism. An example suffices.

*

A student went to his guru for advice and was told to look for the *Atman*, or one Lord, in everything that he met. Not long afterwards he was walking along a road when a very large elephant approached, ridden by a mahout. There was no room for the man and the elephant to pass without danger of an accident. However, the man recalled his guru's advice and remembered the *Atman*. The mahout shouted at him to get out of the way, but the man said to himself, 'The *Atman* is in the elephant; how can the *Atman* hurt me, who also am the *Atman*?' So he continued on his way. On reaching him the elephant seized him with his trunk, and threw him violently to the side of the road. Painfully, the man picked himself up and limped away. Next day he went to his guru and complained indignantly that he had been misled. He recounted the story and expostulated that the guru's advice had failed to protect him. 'Ah!' said the guru, 'but you did not obey when the mahout called to you. You forgot that the *Atman* was in the mahout also.'

Chapter 2

Knowledge and Ignorance

Two kinds of knowledge

'What is knowledge?' asks Arjuna in the *Gita*. Krishna replies that it is to know the field and the knower of the field (XIII, 1–2). What does this strange answer mean? The field refers to everything that can be perceived, in the widest sense of perception. In short, it is everything that is knowable. Thus all that may be experienced through the five senses and all that may be imagined, thought, felt or otherwise experienced inwardly is included in the field. But then if, as Krishna says, knowledge also means to know the knower of the field, then that would also be amongst the knowable, so that would be part of the field too. The solution of this dilemma is that the knower of the field is not knowable. How then can one know something which is not knowable? This question goes to the heart of the philosophy of Vedanta. Before answering it we need to look at other aspects of knowledge.

Owing perhaps to our predominantly scientific culture, in the West we tend to associate knowledge with what can be known empirically or through experience. What we learn with our eyes and ears, such as the fact that it is raining, or that litmus paper turns red in acidic solutions, is regarded as knowledge. So too is what can be learned through extensions of our senses in the form of scientific instruments, like microscopes or particle accelerators, since there is always some actual sense observation involved, such as reading information off a screen.

We also usually consider our inner experience to be part of what we know, even though the precision required for scientific knowledge is lacking. Thus we would say that we know how we feel, what we are thinking or what we can remember of our past lives. Western philosophers, notably Wittgenstein, have challenged this concept of introspective knowledge on the grounds that, for example, I can validly say that I have a pain, but not that I know that I have a pain. Since to know something implies at least the possibility of making a mistake about it, then I cannot know that I have a pain, for I cannot be mistaken. Such an argument leads to the paradoxical conclusion that I can know that someone else has a pain, but not that I have one! However, all this is somewhat beside the point to a Vedantist. It is sufficient for his purposes to say that 'I have a pain' is a case of a field – the pain – and a knower of the field, namely 'I'.

There are, of course, further areas beyond simple empirical experience, whether external or internal, which a Western philosopher might call knowledge. Mathematics is an obvious example, for few would regard its true propositions as empirical. Whether they are truths known intuitively, by analysis or whatever, again the Vedantist can take a firm stand on placing them within the field. Someone who knows Pythagoras' theorem, or the proof of a quadratic equation, knows something within the field. The same goes for someone who knows the truth of a valid proposition in logic, or the definition of a word as given by a dictionary, neither of which is an empirical truth. 'Knowable', therefore, in the sense of whatever is within the field, has a very wide range, and certainly includes all kinds of knowledge which human beings may discover in the future.

The distinction that Krishna makes, however, between the field and the knower of the field is quite different from all the distinctions referred to above. It is not a distinction between outward empirical knowledge and inner introspective knowledge, nor between knowledge from experience and non-experiential, or a priori, knowledge, nor between empirical and logical, or analytic, knowledge. All these are within the field.

If we look more precisely at Krishna's answer, we find that the Sanskrit says something like 'to know the field and the knower of the field, that is the real knowledge.' In other words, he suggests that there are two kinds of knowledge, a higher and a lower. The latter is simply to know the field; the former is to know oneself as the knower of the field. This is confirmed elsewhere in the *Gita* and throughout Vedantic literature. As the modern Vedantist Nikhilananda wrote, 'Self-knowledge is vital. All other forms of knowledge are of secondary importance.' They cover more or less everything that we would call knowledge in the Western world. Psychologists and similar investigators of the mind, or psyche, might object on the grounds that they study and discover knowledge of the self. But do they? Their field of investigation – the phrase is significant – is the contents of the mind, of the emotions and of the imagination, however deeply they penetrate these. How can the Vedantist be so sure of this? The reason is that the self is not to be discovered by looking into the mind, but by finding that which is itself aware of the mind, the knower of the field.

The contrast between higher and lower knowledge is strikingly put in the *Katha* Upanishad:

> 'God made sense turn outward, man therefore looks outward, not into himself. Now and again a daring soul, desiring immortality, has looked back and found himself.'
> (*The Ten Principal Upanishads*, p. 33)

This passage does not simply refer to the five senses turning outwards to the spatial world. The 'sense' that turns outwards includes the sense of inner experience, thoughts and feelings and so on, for these are 'outside' the perceiving or knowing self. The 'daring soul' is the man who wants real self-knowledge, who wants to know the knower of the field.

Yet this fundamental dichotomy between higher and lower knowledge appears to lead to an infinite regression. If the higher knowledge is to know the knower, then who is he who knows the knower? Is he not the knower of the knower? But then real knowledge would be to know this (second) knower, and so on *ad infinitum*. Not so, says the Vedantist. For to know the knower is not to cognize an object. The knower of the field can never be an object, for he is the ultimate subject. How then can he be known? We have returned to the key question with which we began.

The higher knowledge, or self-knowledge, is not a case of becoming aware of an object, as happens with empirical knowledge and also with a priori or analytic knowledge. Yet it is knowledge. To know the knower is to realize that one is the knower, to say 'I know' in full awareness that this is not an act of recognizing something external to oneself, but simply the condition of realizing oneself as a knower. Knowledge is said to be of the nature of the self. As the *Brihadaranyaka* Upanishad puts it, 'The knower's function of knowing can never be lost.' (*Brihad*, IV iii 30). There does not have to be an object of knowing. Such self-knowledge has been compared to light, present in the universe but without objects to illuminate. Such light would be invisible, yet would exist as completely as when it is 'seen' in the form of illuminated objects.

Even the four Veda are within the field of lower knowledge. The *Mandukya* Upanishad confirms that the Veda is of the highest authority, and yet at the same time asserts that merely to know the Veda is not really to know.

> 'Of these, the lower [knowledge] comprises the Rig Veda, Yajur Veda, Sama Veda, Atharva Veda, the science of pronunciation, etc., the code of rituals, grammar, etymology, metre, and astrology. Then there is the higher [knowledge] by which is realized the Immutable.'
> (*Mandukya* Upanishad, I i5, in *The Eight Upanishads*, Vol. 2, pp. 86–7)

In commenting on this verse, Sankara says that the higher knowledge of the Immutable is imparted only by the Upanishads considered as revealed knowledge, but is not the assemblage of words found in the Upanishads. After mastery of the assemblage of words, the student still requires a teacher and the quality of detachment if the Immutable is to be realized. In short, the meaning of the Upanishads has to be found in practice and not merely learnt.

The unity of knowledge

Although there appears to be a sharp distinction between higher and lower knowledge, ultimately Vedanta does not assert that there are two quite separate types of knowledge. Knowledge is one and resides in the self. How then can we understand the lower knowledge to be knowledge at all? And, if we do not call it knowledge, we are left with much confusion about the difference between knowing a straightforward fact, like 'this book is red,' and not knowing it, or just believing it, or making a mistake about it. Vedanta, however, does not totally abandon the lower knowledge in claiming that only the higher knowledge is real. Its method of solving the problem is broadly to subsume the lower knowledge into the higher.

This can be seen in two ways. Firstly, in the case of, for example, empirical knowledge by means of sense perception, there are three principal elements or constituents: the knower (or subject), the act of knowing (such as seeing), and the thing known (or object). To the ordinary mind, all three have to be present distinctly for knowledge to occur. In other words, take any one of the three away and we do not know anything. To the mind fully trained in Vedanta, however, even this threefold situation of knowing becomes subsumed in the unity of knowledge itself, as an aspect of self. Subject, act and object become one. There is knowledge, but not a separate knower, nor a separate object, nor an act between. It is like the experience people sometimes have, when listening to music, of there being just the music and nothing else, no listener and no listening.

> '. . . or music heard so deeply
> That it is not heard at all, but you are the music
> While the music lasts.'
> (T.S. Eliot, *Four Quartets*, 'The Dry Salvages', V)

Indeed, in any 'act' of perception one might validly ask whether the threefold distinction of subject, act and object is actually present in the situation, or whether the mind is introducing into a single unified experience a division between 'me' and 'it', which gives rise to the apparent trinity. If so, it would follow that the self beyond the mind would not recognize such a form of knowledge. On this analysis then there is only one knowledge, the higher one, and the lower one is a sort of superimposition created by the mind, but dependent upon the real knowledge for its putative knowing.

A second way of understanding the subsuming of the lower knowledge in the higher is more direct. When someone says, 'I do not know', there is something which he does know, namely his own ignorance. He knows that he does not know. Behind his lack of knowledge of, say, an empirical fact, such as the actual colour of a book, lies his recognition that he does not know it. Without this recognition he could not assert, 'I do not know.' This kind of 'background' knowledge is always present. It is the knower's function of knowing which can never be lost. The Sanskrit words *jnana* and *ajnana* indicate this. For the former means knowledge of what (really) exists, and the latter means knowledge of what does not exist, or ignorance. The Sanskrit word *ajnana* literally contains the word for knowledge.

Self-knowledge

There is a rather different perspective on this apparent division of knowledge. The Upanishads and Sankara's *Brahma Sutra Bhasya* pay scant attention to what is commonly regarded nowadays as knowledge. In them even the 'lower' knowledge consists of information and rules about rituals and practices for the attainment of the real knowledge of the self. Chants, hymns, meditations, sacrifices and so on are discussed and clarified as means of purifying the mind and preparing the ground for the realization of the one truth to which all students of Vedanta aspire. Much of this 'lower' knowledge is, in fact, found in the Vedas themselves, rather than in the more philosophical Vedanta. This makes the task of relating Western philosophical ideas to those of Vedanta difficult, since even ancient Greek philosophers, and certainly modern European ones, have had a great deal to say about what the Indian sages did not regard as of any real significance, namely knowledge of the world and of how it operates. For them, to know about the field for its own sake is to miss the point. To know the field and the knower of the field for the sake of the self is the whole point.

Although Vedanta does discuss the five senses, sense objects, the mind and its contents and others aspects of 'lower' knowledge, it does so in order to relate them finally to knowledge of the self. It is this which distinguishes Vedanta from most Western philosophy. Indeed, it is this which makes it of special interest to the Western world at a time when the West is becoming almost totally absorbed with empirical and introspective knowledge, and the worldly benefits of the accumulation of such information. One of the greatest of modern scientists has acknowledged this.

> 'You may ask – you are bound to ask me now: What, then, is in your opinion the value of natural science? I answer: Its scope, aim and value is the same as that of any other branch of human knowledge. Nay, none of them alone, only the union of all of them, has any scope or value at all, and that is simply enough described: it is to obey the command of the Delphic deity . . . know yourself.'
>
> (Erwin Schrödinger, '*Nature and the Greeks*' and '*Science and Humanism*', p. 108)

Sense perception

In modern philosophy, under the influence of the Florentine Renaissance, sense perception has played a central role as the chief means for the acquisition of empirical knowledge of the world, leading to the successful development of science. Locke, Berkeley, Hume and Kant, for example, all had much to say about the status of knowledge derived through the five senses, about the difference between primary qualities, such as extension in space, and secondary qualities, like colour, and about the discovery of empirical laws.

Vedanta, in sharp contrast, shows little interest in the philosophical problems of perception. Hume's problem of ascertaining the causal connection between an observed event and its effect, and Kant's ingenious puzzle about the sequence of our impressions when we watch a boat travel down a river, do not attract the attention of a Vedantist. Why not? – because Vedanta devotes itself to an enquiry into a single question about the world and the self, namely what is real, what truly exists. Since its conclusion – indeed one might say its starting point – is that only the self is real, there is no reason to give undue attention to problems within the field of perception that do not impinge closely upon the proper concern of philosophical investigation.

Yet the literature of Vedanta does discuss what might loosely be called the 'ingredients' of perception. From these it is possible to extract a theory more or less common to a variety of teachers, at least those of the *Advaita* Vedanta tradition. The theory, however, remains entirely subordinate to the one aim. Interest in the mechanics of sense perception, for example, derives entirely from the assistance that understanding them gives to the student seeking the truth about the self.

To make this clearer we need to place these 'ingredients' within a general epistemological scheme. To some extent this must be drawn from accounts in the Upanishads of the whole process of creation, in which elements emerge from the one creative source, the *Brahman*, in temporal progression. The *Taittiriya* Upanishad provides a striking example.

'From that *Brahman*, which is the Self, was produced space.
From space, emerged air. From air was born fire. From
fire was created water. From water, sprang up earth.'

(Taittiriya, II i I, in *The Eight Upanishads*, Vol. I, p. 287)

Sankara, however, treated such accounts as metaphysics, and
eschewed the concept of succession in time, except when he
himself chose to offer creation myths. His commentary on this
extract from the *Taittiriya* points out that *Brahman* is the material cause of elements such as space – in other words, they are
made of *Brahman* (or consciousness), as a pot is made of clay.
Hence the succession of elements is an epistemological one: space
precedes air in the sense that the existence of air necessarily
requires the existence of space, but not vice versa; and the existence of space necessarily requires the existence of consciousness,
and not vice versa.

As it happens, this particular statement in the *Taittiriya* has
aroused debate amongst Vedantists, since it omits the usual succession occurring between *Brahman* and space. In other texts there
are intermediate stages mainly associated with mind, and this is
undoubtedly the purport of the Vedanta doctrine (*see* pp.
147–153). In the context of sense perception, however, it is conven-
ient to limit the discussion to the elements of space, air, fire, water
and earth. These five are associated with the sense organs – ear,
skin, eye, tongue and nose. According to a doctrine taken from
the Samkya system (a non-Vedantic dualistic philosophy with roots
in the Upanishads), and used in the epics and *Puranas* of Vedanta
– though not explicitly in the *Taittiriya* Upanishad – the immediate objects of each sense are not these so-called gross elements,
but rather five corresponding subtle elements (*tanmatra*). This is
not at all as obscure as it may seem. The subtle elements are sound,
touch, colour (or shape), taste and smell. Each is the direct percept
of a sense, in a one to one relationship. Thus the ear perceives
sound, the skin perceives touch and so on. The 18th-century British
idealist philosopher, Bishop George Berkeley, held to the view that

each sense has its own exclusive object, and indeed common sense supports it, for what else can the ear hear but sound – certainly not touch or taste.

THE NINE ELEMENTS

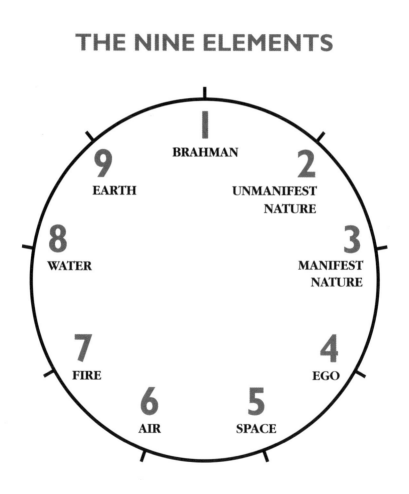

1 BRAHMAN

2 UNMANIFEST NATURE

3 MANIFEST NATURE

4 EGO

5 SPACE

6 AIR

7 FIRE

8 WATER

9 EARTH

On the question of whether more than one sense impression can be experienced at the same time, a nice Vedantic analogy is that impressions are like manuscript leaves which may appear to be pierced simultaneously by a pin, but in fact are run through successively at great speed.

Where then do the five gross elements fit into this scheme? They are, as it were, the building blocks of the material or physical world. From their intermixture are formed gross objects such as bodies and tables. Thus, when we perceive a table, several senses may be operating together. We may see colour and shape in a table-like presentation, feel with the skin the touch of the wood, and even hear the sound of an object striking the table to emit a table-like audible impression. The mind appreciates the discrete subtle elements and interprets the collection, or mixture, as a table made up of gross elements external to itself. They are external precisely because they are in space, the first gross element. (*See* Chapter 10, 'Language', for a further development of this account.)If space is absent, the other gross elements cannot exist. If, in such a case, other subtle elements are present, then the mind understands that what is perceived is interior or, as we might say, imagined or dreamt. Space itself can be imagined, so that there may be the experience of a table, but not in actual three-dimensional space. For this reason Vedanta treats the senses themselves as distinct from the sense organs. The latter are the physical ear, etc., in themselves objects made up of gross elements. They provide us with experience of things outside ourselves. The senses, on the other hand, are subtle organs, which operate internally, both when things are imagined and when they are actually there in space. Again this is a fairly simple and commonsense view. If one is looking at a table and then closes the eyes, an image of the table may remain in the mind's eye for a while. In other words, 'seeing' continues, much as it did when the eyes were open. If we call this seeing a subtle organ, then the subtle organ, as it were, penetrates the gross organ of the eye and sees either externally or internally, according to whether the eyelids are raised or not. Similarly, the direct object of the subtle organ (colour and shape in this case) is present in both instances. Only the gross element is absent when the eyes are closed.

However, there is an inconsistency in this account. Imagined space is not easily regarded as sound – the subtle element corresponding to gross space does not seem to be the 'container' of the other elements in a way analogous to the containment of the other four gross elements by physical space. A partial reconciliation can be effected by regarding 'sound' as rather like the element ether, which until the 20th century was regarded as a 'very rarefied and highly elastic substance (formerly) believed to permeate all space' (*Oxford Dictionary of English*). After all, we do not regard 'inner' space as actually three-dimensional, so perhaps it can be thought of as a kind of ethereal substance akin to sound.

Indeed the idea of subtle elements and senses raises further possibilities. Why should we not consider all five senses to have an inner dimension that has greater scope than simply the ability to imagine things? We regularly use phrases like 'being in touch' and 'having a taste for something' to refer to quite subtle inner experiences. We are inclined to regard all such uses as metaphors or analogues of the 'real' senses, ignoring perhaps that this assumes the greater reality of the physical world. It may be that we should regard them as epistemologically more fundamental than the gross senses. Perhaps our sense of inner space influences, or even determines, our sense of outer space. It is a common feeling that we have space to think or feel, that our inner world is freer or less constricted, and usually this is projected on to our awareness of outer space. Similarly, a person who has 'good taste', who selects with care what is of finer quality by reference to an inner sense, is likely to be fastidious about what food he or she eats.

The relationship between gross and subtle senses is sometimes expressed in Vedanta as though the gross sense conveys the subtle sense to the mind. Such a view is most intelligible in the important case of the first element, space. Science assures us that sound waves are conveyed through a medium, albeit air rather than space itself. Again we may look back to the old concept of ether, which was removed from modern science as a result of an experiment dealing with the transmittance, not of sound, but of light. The conveyance of touch by air is in keeping with our experience of air on the skin and perhaps with the general sensitivity of the sense of touch. Fire as a gross element is frequently identified with light in Vedic literature, and there is no doubt that light is the conveyor of colour and shape. Similarly water, in the generic form of liquid, conveys taste. As for earth and smell, where the relationship is more obscure, science again comes to our aid, in so far as smell is transmitted by tiny physical particles entering the nose.

An assessment of the theory of sense perception

In summary, the Vedantic account of sense perception is that knowledge (of the lower type) arises when a gross sense organ is in contact with a gross object. The latter is composed of a group of gross elements, which embody or convey subtle elements. The senses themselves experience the subtle elements, which are passed to the mind for co-ordination and interpretation. Later on more will be said about *manas*, the aspect of mind which performs these functions (*see* pp. 149–150).

How then does this explanation stand up to the kinds of questions asked by Western philosophers about perception? Firstly, what of the famous criticism levelled at Berkeley: that if 'to be is to be perceived', do chairs and tables exist when no one is perceiving them (Berkeley himself answered by claiming – as a bishop – that God perceived everything always!) Sankara is very insistent, in arguing against Buddhists, about the difference between perceptions and the things perceived.

> 'Something other than the perception has to be admitted perforce, just because it is perceived. Not that anybody cognizes a perception to be a pillar, a wall, etc, rather all people cognize a pillar, a wall, etc. as objects of percep-

tion ... Accordingly, those who accept truth to be just
what it is actually perceived to be, should accept a thing
as it actually reveals itself externally, and not "as though
appearing outside."'

(*Brahma Sutra Bhasya*, p. 419)

Gross elements exist regardless of the presence or absence of
human perception of them, and *a fortiori* the material objects
composed of them also exist when they are not perceived. Yet the
gross elements seem to be merely impressions at the end of a
kind of individual chain, beginning with the individual self and
passing through the mind and the subtle senses. How is this
dilemma to be resolved?

Here we must turn to the higher knowledge. *Brahman*
permeates everything that exists. It is the material cause of the
world. Nothing exists without the presence of *Brahman*. Hence
the individual self and all its organs and functions are forms or
manifestations of the same substance, the consciousness which
is *Brahman*.

The grossness of the gross elements is only relative, for they
partake of the same substance as the subtle elements. Even the
individual self, which seems to be the ultimate perceiver, is in itself
nothing other than *Brahman*. Each item in the 'chain' of perception emerges, as it were, from *Brahman*, however much it may
appear that they follow each other in a kind of causal sequence
within, and exterior to, an individual. In short, if someone shuts
his eyes, the table he saw continues to exist, because it arises from
universal consciousness, not from his particular subtle impressions
of it. In principle this is not unlike Berkeley's answer, but it is
supported by philosophical assumptions and arguments peculiar
to Vedanta, which we shall consider later.

A corollary to this reply is that both the gross and subtle
elements are, in Platonic terms, universals. Air, for example, is one;
so too is touch. There are not a multitude of airs or touches each
corresponding to an individual experience. Each experience may

be unique – may differ in detail from every other experience. One touch may be hard, another soft and so on, but all are just the one subtle element of touch. As elsewhere in Vedanta, Plato's concept helps our understanding. Universals have no parts. What seem to be their parts are really instances of them in particular situations. Hence a hard touch is a hard instance of touch, not a part of touch which is hard.

Nor does Wittgenstein's theory of family resemblances apply here. Touch is definitely not a case of family resemblance whereby there is nothing in common between all experiences of touch, and only overlapping resemblances between any two or more. The one element touch is present in every case of touching. What follows from this, amongst other things, is that each element, both gross and subtle, is intrinsically pure, even when it is intermixed with others to form an object. Apparent impurities are simply examples of ignorance on the part of the perceiver.

In light of all this we might wonder whether we ever see objects at all. Despite Sankara's assertion, surely we are aware of sense data, or impressions made upon our sense organs, and not of any actual object existing independently of our perception of it? Modern Western philosophy, of course, has had a great deal to say about this. One way in which Vedanta deals with this is by recourse to language. Objects, so called, are the creation of words. A word does not merely stick a label on a perceived object. On the contrary, the perceived object exists only in so far as a word, sounding in the consciousness which is its source, gives it a form in the physical world. As the *Chandogya* Upanishad puts it:

> 'All transformation has speech as its basis, and it is name only.'
>
> (*Chandogya* Upanishad, VI i4, p. 409)

Suppose a black speck is seen in the sky. When it becomes larger it is identified as an aeroplane. Then we see that it is a Boeing 747, and finally identify it as the plane that arrives from New York at midday. We believe that it is the same object throughout, as though we have merely changed its labels. But that is from the standpoint of belief in a physical world of objects in space, existing independently of our descriptions, which is the very question at issue. That whole standpoint is a product of language. Successive descriptions in words have created a series of sense experiences, which the mind interprets as the independent movement of a single object, namely the plane from New York. What then of the black speck? Did that not exist as a kind of basic object, upon which words were imposed? Obviously not – 'black' and 'speck' are words also, which create black specks! Thus there can be no experience of an objective world without knowledge or use of language. What then do animals perceive? If you pursue questions too far, says one Upanishad, your head will fall off! (Nevertheless, *see* Chapter 10, 'Language', for further discussion.)

Measure in sense perception

Somewhat paradoxically, in view of this doctrine of sense perception, Vedanta refers to the senses as organs of knowledge. Yet, like Plato, Sankara regards sense perception as liable to error, and as a potentially destructive force.

> 'Things of sense are more penetrating in the hurt they cause than the venom of the black serpent. The poison slays only him into whom it enters, but things of sense destroy through mere beholding.'
>
> (*The Crest Jewel of Wisdom*, p. 22)

How can the senses be both organs of knowledge and a form of poison, for nowhere does Vedanta regard knowledge as harmful? The answer lies in the use made of the sense organs. Sense perception only occurs in the present moment, not in the past or future. If the imagination plays with past and future sensual images, there are repercussions. Used merely for pleasure, or for the selfish ends of the perceiver, the senses are destructive.

There is a traditional story of a man who grossly abused the sense of taste. He was offered sweets by a wealthy associate, who gave him money for each sweet eaten. The greedy man ate the sweets, until his stomach was near to bursting. He had to be carried home, as he was unable to walk. Whereupon a doctor was called, who prescribed a pill. But the greedy man gasped that he could not swallow the pill. 'If I had room for the pill,' he said, 'I should have eaten another sweet!'

Such greed displays a total lack of measure. A serious student of Vedanta, searching for the truth, uses the sense organs under the guidance of reason, and therefore measures out their use to the needs of the body, the mind, and indeed of the world. Feeding the senses with impressions is like pouring butter on fire. Fire is never satisfied; it will consume butter indefinitely. So, too, will each sense 'consume' its own appropriate impressions – such as colour and shape for the eye – without restraint, unless reason intervenes. What is the measure? In practice, not in theory, reason finds the measure for each sense, usually with reference to the need at the time. 'How much land does a man need?', asked Leo Tolstoy. Any more is greed and causes trouble.

Vedantic tradition ascribes to each sense a presiding god, who controls or rules over it – for instance the Sun (*Surya*) over the eye; the Wind (*Vayu*) over the skin. Rationalist philosophers have interpreted this as a kind of direction not to misuse the senses, since each has an inner nature or essence directing the outcome of their use or abuse. When the eye is overworked or strained, it malfunctions, or even goes blind. Whether this is the punishment of the gods or the operation of nature does not greatly affect the consequences for the unfortunate owner of the eye.

If the senses are measured out in their use, then they are instruments of knowledge. For it is a cardinal precept of Vedanta that a measured (rational) life is conducive to realization of the truth. Knowledge from sense experience is not, therefore, an end in itself in the form of accumulating empirical information, nor even a means to the growth of science, but rather a method of penetrating the world of sense objects in order to find what is 'behind' them. Firstly, there are the pure gross elements – space,

air, fire (light), water and earth – then the pure subtle elements
– sound, touch, colour and shape, taste and smell – then the mind
with its own constituent elements; and finally the conscious self,
which alone is real. For ultimately the world of sense perception
is unreal, not in the sense of not existing at all, but of having no
existence independent of the consciousness that sustains it. In the
final analysis the world is ephemeral, whilst the self is everlasting.

Ordinary ignorance

Unlike some Buddhist schools of philosophy, for whom perception consists merely in the experience of sense impressions devoid
of objects existing in the world, Vedanta in general, and Sankara
in particular, makes a distinction between perception of objects in
the world and the occurrence of dream objects, imagined objects
or mistaken objects. There is a difference, he asserts, between the
perception of things and the things themselves. The sight of a tree
is not itself a tree; the touch of fur is not itself fur, even though
in each case the former appears to be dependent upon the latter.

Sankara's criteria for making this distinction would be
perfectly acceptable to most modern Western philosophers. There
must be spatial, temporal and causal conditions which are adequate
for an object to exist, if there is to be perception of something.
In other words, the thing must be observed to be in a spatial location, to occur in an intelligible time sequence, and to be in a determinate causal relationship with other appropriate things or events.
Finally, the object must not be sublated arbitrarily, as when a dream
object totally disappears when the dreamer awakes, or when it
changes abruptly into something else, as in a dream. (Quantum
physics postulates such changes, but not as a matter of direct
perception.) Thus Sankara says that a dream chariot cannot exist
in space, because there is no room inside the body of the dreamer
for it. Nor can a dreaming man reach a real place hundreds of
miles away and return within the few minutes that a dream lasts.
Likewise, normal causal relations and continuity of objects do not
occur in most dreams.

These arguments are not conclusive. Within the dream world there is dream space, dream time and a kind of dream causality and continuity, all of which seem to possess a validity of their own. To shorten the consideration of this problem, however, we might introduce an aphorism of Wittgenstein's in defence of Sankara – 'to imagine a doubt is not to doubt'. Which of us actually doubts that dreams are unreal and the waking world real? We can all imagine that we doubt this, but do we really doubt it? If asked to choose between being chased by a tiger and being chased by a dream tiger, we would have no doubts!

Ignorance of the self

Vedanta is not too concerned about such elusive problems. Ignorance in relation to the lower knowledge is one thing. Ignorance of what is real is another. Indeed the former is best utilized as an analogy for the latter. For example, one sees a snake on the path ahead, but it turns out merely to be a stick. One could use up a great deal of mental energy in answering such questions as 'Did the illusory snake exist?', 'If not, what is it?', 'How could the "snake" have been different from the stick?' and so on. Vedanta, however, keeps its eye on the target of the truth itself. The mistaken stick stands for the whole world of objects, both in space and in the mind. Philosophical ignorance believes that this world is fundamentally real, that we are born into it and later die, that we are separate selves who perceive objects in the world outside us, and so on. On the other hand, the higher knowledge sees the mistake, or rather does not make it. This so-called world, viewed correctly – as a stick and not as a snake – is one with the self. The self contains it, just as the spatial world for Kant exists transcendentally, but not empirically, in us.

The student of Vedanta, if not interested overmuch in empirical mistakes, does investigate transcendental mistakes. To mistake the self for the world is such a huge and widespread error on the part of mankind that it needs to be examined, if only in order to help eradicate it. Why is the error made? What are the causes of this deeply rooted ignorance? Sometimes it is described as the 'disease of the world'. Medical analogies have been used: a man with an eye disease has double vision, or sees things in a confused way. The remedy is to treat the organ of the eye, to remove a cataract, to repair a torn retina or whatever. Then the man sees clearly. In himself, as the perceiver or observer, he has no disease, no impediment. As soon as the organ is repaired, he sees what is actually there in front of him. So too, says Sankara, the ordinary man thinks that he sees an objective world. His disease, or the impediments to his knowing the truth, are in the mind. Ideas of duality, especially of 'me and the world', stand between himself and the so-called world. If these are removed, then he knows himself as the world and the world as himself. There is unity in place of duality.

In order to remove such ideas, firstly they must be observed. Instead of forming a kind of unnoticed screen, filtering everything that is perceived, they must be recognized as mere ideas. This alone may not remove them. Practice is necessary. The teacher may suggest better ideas to substitute for the false ones, such as 'All this is *Brahman*', or 'Not this, not this', which denies the reality of the world external to the self and then denies the separate self which thinks it is the denier. Or he may recommend detachment from 'objects', especially from those to which one is especially attracted, like food, fine clothes or sex. Or he may advocate measure in the use of the senses. All of these weaken the impediments to knowledge. Many, if not all, of them are driven by desire; hence the need for practices which may involve a degree of austerity. Behind them, however, stands the fundamental impediment – the idea of duality. One cure removes this once and for all: knowledge itself.

Ignorance can have no effect upon the self. The stick seen as a snake cannot bite the man; the water of the mirage in the desert does not moisten the soil. Yet a puzzle remains concerning ignorance of the self. Whose is it? Who or what is ignorant? 'By whomsoever it is seen', replies one guru. But, he adds, there is no point in asking further who that is, since when it is clearly seen it is no longer possessed. Ignorance is merely the absence of discrimination, the failure to distinguish between the field and the knower of the field.

Chapter 3

The Self

The individual self

Ten men on a journey came to a river. They swam across, and once on the further bank they counted to ensure that all had survived. Each time they counted the answer was nine. When they concluded that one had drowned, they wept at the loss of one of their number. A wise man happened to meet them, and enquired why they were lamenting. They said that one of their friends had drowned. He told them to stand in a line. Then he counted them, tapping each on the shoulder in turn with his stick. Finally he tapped the last man and pronounced them to be ten in number. Happy that none were lost, they thanked him and went on their way.

What is the point of this traditional story of Vedanta? It is that each man had forgotten to count himself. The wise man reminded each one of his own self. Superficially this might be seen as a rather unnecessary instruction. Do we not remember ourselves only too much? Most of us are habitually rather selfish. We think of our own likes and dislikes a great deal. We do what we want, rather than give way to the interests of others. We prefer ourselves to others in much of our daily life. Would we not be better advised to remember others, rather than ourselves?

Such an interpretation makes the assumption that we know

who or what we are. It also assumes that to know our likes, desires, needs and preferences is to know who has them. Yet even a cursory examination of the question makes it clear that we are not simply equivalent to what we have in the way of likes, desires, and so on. For one thing, if we *were* them, then indeed we would be hydra-headed monsters with as many selves as we have such inclinations. What the wise man revealed was that we ignore the self that we really are – the true self.

Self in Western philosophy

So who or what is this true self? Western philosophers have given much thought to this question. David Hume's investigation is justifiably famous.

> 'For my part, when I enter most intimately into what I call *myself*, I always stumble on some particular perception or other, of heat or cold, light or shade, love or hatred, pain or pleasure. I never catch *myself* at any time without a perception, and never can observe anything but the perception.'
>
> (A *Treatise of Human Nature*, Book I, iv, vi)

What is at issue is the conclusion that follows from Hume's observation. Kant was – as he put it – 'woken from his dogmatic slumber' by Hume's denial of the self as a substance, and was provoked to conceive the idea of the transcendental unity of apperception. Such a principle asserts that the self has – or perhaps is – a necessary unity, without which human experience as the object of a single conscious subject would be completely unintelligible. Gilbert Ryle, on the other hand, inferred from Hume that the self is not the kind of thing that can be discovered by introspection, and that to look for it in that way is a mistake.

Existentialist writers, such as Sartre and Camus – not perhaps influenced directly by Hume – have exhibited a kind of existential fear. Characters in such novels as *La Nausée* and *L'Étranger* have come to realize that they do not know who they are, and consequently they have been confronted with a deep sense of non-existence, a bottomless gulf of unreality. This metaphysical emptiness became itself a subject for intellectual analysis; for example, in Sartre's examination of nothingness.

In so far as Vedanta uses a method of negation in enquiring into the self, it is not unlike these trends of Western thought. The instruction to say 'Not this, not this' to any feature of oneself which can be observed drives the student of Vedanta back upon himself by denying that he is any of the observed phenomena. He observes his own body, so he is not that. He observes his thoughts and imaginings, so he is not those. He observes his feelings and emotions, his desires, his attitudes, his deeply rooted ideas about the world, other people and himself, his idea of himself as a subject of experience, his ideas of himself as the observer – to all these he says, 'Not this, not this.' It may be that such a far-reaching exercise in negation could indeed lead to a state of nothingness, or at least to a conviction of one's own non-existence. But Vedanta does not stop there. It destroys false beliefs in the self only in order to reveal, not another belief, even a true one, but the realization of what *actually* exists.

The justification for the procedure of negation rests upon a very simple principle. The student begins with a commonsense distinction between subject and object. Vedanta adopts the student's standpoint in order to guide him towards the truth from his own starting place. He is the subject. An object is perceived – the body, for example. The principle applied is that the object itself cannot be the subject – 'I am not this body being observed.' And this process continues with each successive object, even as far as the idea that one is an observing subject, for that too, as an idea, can be observed. Yet the subject, as subject, can never be observed.

Again this conclusion is what Hume was pointing out in his introspective experiment. However, commentators like Ryle have interpreted it as a matter of logic – by definition a subject cannot be an object. But in this instance more than logic is at stake.

Whatever may be taken as subject and object, it would be a logical error to confuse them. Equally, it would be logically correct to ensure that whatever is regarded as subject observes what is regarded as object. Hence there is no logical error in saying that the mind observes the body. Yet this may be an error of fact. It may not actually be the case that the mind observes the body, for perhaps the mind is no more than an instrument whereby the self – the real observer – observes the body. Similarly, it is a logical error to think that the self can itself be observed, but to avoid the logical error is not the end of the enquiry; it is the beginning of it. Not that Western philosophers have always made this error: Hume, Ryle, Sartre and others have developed quite elaborate theories about the self, but this is not the place to examine them.

The self as spirit

Vedanta accepts this logical introduction to the enquiry into the self. Self as subject should never be confused with any object. Anything that the self observes cannot be the self. Can anything positive then be said of it? The *Brihadaranyaka* Upanishad has a great deal to say about the self. For example:

> 'This Self is nearer than all else; dearer than son, dearer than wealth, dearer than anything. If a man call anything dearer than the Self, say that he will lose what is dear; of a certainty he will lose it; for the Self is God. Therefore one should worship Self as Love. Who worships Self as Love, his love never shall perish ... This Self is the Lord of all beings; as all spokes are knit together in the hub, all things, all gods, all men, all lives, all bodies, are knit together in that Self.'

> (pp. 121, 135)

> 'He wanted every form, for He wanted to show Himself; as a magician He appears in many forms, he masters hundreds and thousands of powers. He is those powers;

those millions of powers, those innumerable powers. He
is Spirit; without ante-cedent, without precedent, without
inside, without outside; omnipresent, omniscient. Self is
Spirit. That is revelation.'

(p. 136)

The connection between these two passages lies in the assertion
that self is spirit. Self is dear, self is to be worshipped, self is love,
because it is spirit. What can be observed is material. Things in
space, including human bodies, are material, made of the gross
elements; things in the mind are subtle, made of finer material and
observable as imagined objects or as thoughts, feelings and
emotions; but the witness of them all, of all materiality, is of a
different order. It is spirit. To know that spirit is revelation. To know
that spirit is not to know an object; it is to realize that one is spirit.

Ramana Maharshi on the self
Lest it be thought that Vedanta tips over at this point into religion,
so that anyone who denies, or even doubts, the existence of God
cannot follow the enquiry into self any further, it is useful to turn
to a modern exponent of Vedanta, whose teaching about the self
was often expressed without any religious connotations at all.
Ramana Maharshi, after many years of severe austerities, came to
a sudden realization of the truth of *Advaita* Vedanta. As a teacher
he attracted many students from around the world, those from
the West perhaps being drawn by his simple, undogmatic style of
instruction. Every question was referred by him to the self. For
example, one of his favourite devices, when dealing with apparently daunting enquiries about, for example, the creation of the
universe, or the purpose of life, was to ask, 'Who wants to know
that?' His intention was to reveal to the student that his or her
question might originate in some state of mind not relevant to a
real enquiry into the self. Looking at the source of the question
enabled the questioner to say 'Not this' to it, which is one step
nearer to the self.

Ramana Maharshi's prosaic approach, which was acceptable to people of all faiths, or of none at all, was demonstrated in answering a question about religion.

> 'People would not understand the simple and bare truth – the truth of their every day, ever-present and eternal experience. That Truth is that of the Self. Is there anyone not aware of the Self? They would not even like to hear it [the Self], whereas they are eager to know what lies beyond – heaven, hell, reincarnation. Because they love mystery and not the bare truth, religions pamper them – only to bring them round to the Self. Wandering hither and thither you must return to the Self only. Then, why not abide in the Self even here and now?'
>
> (*Talks with Sri Ramana Maharshi*, p. 131)

For the Vedantist, the self, though the dearest of all, to be loved above all else, is not remote, other-worldly or unattainable. It is here and now, in this world, at this time, the nearest thing of all. What could be nearer than oneself? The problem is merely that we forget it. Our lives are spent being identified with what we like and dislike, with what we are doing, with our states of mind and body, with other people. We think 'I am thirsty', 'I am tired', 'I am good at my job', 'I am useless at doing this', 'I am in love with X', 'I am hated by Y'. In truth, I am none of these. In believing that I am them, I have forgotten that I am just myself and nothing else. The Sanskrit language makes this very clear. *Aham* means 'I am'. *Ahankara* means 'I am something' – an action, a thought, a feeling. We habitually identify 'I' with what we do. Vedanta says in a cryptic aphorism, 'I do nothing at all'. To realize the self is to know that I do nothing at all. I am the witness of what is done, the ultimate observer. Nor does a witness act, any more than a mirror acts in reflecting what is before it. An illustration by Ramana Maharshi emphasizes that forgetfulness is at the root of philosophical error.

'A lady had a precious necklace round her neck. Once in
her excitement she forgot it and thought that the necklace
was lost. She became anxious and looked for it in her home
but could not find it. She asked her friends and neighbours
if they knew anything about the necklace. They did not.
At last a kind friend of hers told her to feel the necklace
round the neck. She found that it had all along been round
her neck and she was happy! When others asked her later
if she found the necklace which was lost, she said, "Yes, I
have found it." She still felt that she had recovered a lost
jewel. Now did she lose it at all? It was all along round her
neck. But judge her feelings. She is happy as if she had
recovered a lost jewel. Similarly with us, we imagine that
we would realise that Self some time, whereas we are
never anything but the Self.'

(*Talks*, p. 588)

The 'lost' jewel is the same as the 'lost' tenth man in the story of
crossing the river. Neither were really lost, both were unnoticed
or forgotten. Philosophy in the tradition of Vedanta has the task
of reminding the student of the self. How strange that we need
such reminders!

The universal self

What could be more individual than the self? Surely each person is
unique. Even human bodies have unique characteristics; no two faces
are identical; the number of variable features that each body has –
height, weight, shape, colour of hair – is so great that they alone
guarantee the uniqueness of each combination. As for the mind, how
different we all are in character, personality, intelligence, emotional
responses and so on. Indeed, the amazing fact is that of the some
six billion people alive at present no two are the same, not even
'identical' twins. Yet Vedanta claims that there is a universal self. But
is the self not the least likely thing of all to be the same in everyone?

Before proceeding further, the ambiguity of the word 'same' needs to be addressed. If I have the same car as my neighbour, this means that we each have an Opel Zafira 1.8 litre, perhaps of the same colour. In other words, we have the same kind of car. We do not have identically the same car. Or if we did, I would say that I share a car with my neighbour. On the other hand, in a court case an advocate might consider it essential to establish that a car used by his client was, or was not, the very same car as the one seen at a certain time and place by a witness. Hence 'same' may mean 'same kind' or 'identically (or numerically) the same', according to the context.

If we were to say that the existence of a universal self means only that human beings all have the same kind of self – a human self, or a conscious self – the statement would be a platitude, except perhaps in the minds of some racists or Marxists. Vedanta, of course, does not say this (though it certainly does not deny it!). It asserts that there is a self which is identically the same in each person. That is why the claim seems so preposterous, especially to the Western mind brought up in a culture of what is loosely called 'individualism'.

While discussing the meaning of words, it will be helpful to look briefly at a relevant feature of the French language. French uses the word '*même*' for both 'self' and 'same'. *Moi-même* means 'I myself'; *toi-même* means 'you yourself' and so on. Yet *même* also means 'same' in the straightforward sense of sameness. *La même voiture* means 'the same car'.

The analogy of space

An argument by analogy that is often used in the Upanishads to support the concept of a universal self compares it to space. A room, in a sense, contains space. So does a jar, or any container. From the standpoint of a person in a room or of a fly in a bottle, the interior space is separate from the space outside, and might be regarded as an individual space. Indeed sociologists often talk of the difference between public space and private space, as though the latter included instances of individual spaces. However, we all know that in reality space is one. How we know this is a difficult question. While Kant said it is by intuition, his view of space was perhaps unduly influenced by Newtonian mechanics. Today, Western philosophers, influenced by Einstein, might regard it as a theoretical concept. How space is measured is another related difficulty. Since space is now regarded by physicists to be measurable only with reference to the velocity of light travelling in space, rather than by absolutely fixed measuring rods, it can no longer be seen as a sort of unchanging container in which events happen that have no bearing on its qualities.

However, none of these problems of knowing about space need affect our justifiable conviction that space is one. The space in a jar is the same space as that outside the jar. We are tempted to say that it is part of the one space, but even that is questionable. A part has limits, but so-called 'parts' of space have no limits at all. Space is utterly seamless. Jars, of course, are limits, but they do not limit space – they merely limit the things genuinely contained in them, such as air or wine. When a jar is moved, the space inside does not move around with the jar, whereas the air or wine does. So when we speak of parts of space, strictly we are not referring to parts of a gross substance like the parts of a quantity of water, or the parts of a machine.

What has this to do with the self? According to Vedanta, the universal self is like space. It has no limits, however much people think it has. Human bodies and minds may seem to contain it, but they no more do so than a jug contains space. After all, if the self is contained in the body, then a surgeon could find it. Perhaps he cannot do so because it is invisible; but then if it is imperceptible to all five senses, why should we expect to find it within a very perceptible thing like a human body? We do not expect to find non-perceptible things, such as numbers (as opposed to the numerals which denote them) inside the head of, say, a mathematician, or indeed inside anything. Non-spatial things cannot be located.

A Platonic argument about the self

Like space, then, argues Vedanta, the self is one. Yet we ordinarily regard each human being as a conscious self. Certainly every person has consciousness, but leaving aside for the present questions about being unconscious or asleep, is this consciousness a unique possession of an individual, so that each is justified in saying 'my consciousness'? Obviously people do say this, but what do they actually mean by it, and are they really being coherent in saying it? Is 'my consciousness' just a rarefied example from amongst all the things that we own, rather like our much less rarefied body, or an even less rarefied car? An argument on the lines of that used for the unity of space might again be deployed. What intrinsic limits are there to consciousness, as opposed to limits on a single human body or mind?

This argument may be reinforced by the kind of Platonic view of universals referred to earlier when discussing the elements. Consciousness is a universal, such that the consciousness of one person is not an individual part of consciousness, but rather an instance of it in a part of the human race. For the human race – if not humanity itself – has parts in the form of individual people, identifiable by highly distinctive bodies and minds. Hence each person demonstrates an instance of the one universal consciousness, but this is not to say that each person contains a part of consciousness, any more than the whiteness of a part is a part of whiteness. Such a Platonic conclusion is drawn simply to reveal a little more of what Vedanta means by a universal self. This is especially relevant in so far as that self is said to be of the nature of consciousness, existence and bliss, each of which is universal and ultimately no different from the unity of the self itself.

Self in the *Gita* and the Upanishads

In striking contrast to such scholastic arguments, the *Bhagavad Gita* offers a poetic account of the universal self, which appeals more to the emotions than to the intellect. This self is found everywhere.

'I am Lord Visnu of the seven gods
Amidst the stars I am resplendent Sun,
And Moon amongst the other heavenly orbs;
I am the flash of lightening in the storm.
I am the *Sama* of the Vedic songs,
And I am Indra, Lord of all the gods.
I am the mind controlling every sense
And pure intelligence in all that lives.

. . .

I am the ocean, greatest of the seas,
And I am Bhrgu, father of the wise.
Of words I am the single sound of OM;
Of offerings I am the sacrifice
In silent repetition in the mind;
And, of unmoving things, Himalaya;
Of trees, I am the holy Asvattha;
And Narada amongst the godly seers.
Of those who play the music of the gods
I am Citraratha; and Kapila
Of holy saints; and know Me as the horse
Uccaisravas, who rose like nectar from
The churning sea; of elephants I am
Airayata, and, of all men, the king.'
                    (X, 21–22, 24–27, pp. 88–9)

In this way the *Gita* portrays the universal self as immanent in all things, as the spirit of the world, animating all that lives, residing even in the rocks of the earth, in the heavens and in the souls of men. To those who can respond to such a conception, the arguments of philosophy may become redundant. Yet an emotional response may not always be forthcoming, so that, like St Anselm, we may need intellectual understanding to complement our faith in a being which is transcendent as well as immanent.

In the *Eesha* Upanishad the universal self, or *Brahman*, is described as transcendent. All created things are 'covered' by this transcendent self. The Sanskrit word meaning transcendent is *paribhuh*, meaning literally 'being beyond or around'. This self does not extend in space beyond all things in space; it extends beyond space itself. Nor does it endure before and after all things in time; it endures beyond time itself. All things in time and space are born from, exist in virtue of, and dissolve into *Brahman*, the universal self, for *Brahman* is the womb or matrix of time and space, and hence of absolutely everything therein. The *Brihadaranyaka*, with some irony, puts this idea across in a conversation between a pupil, Gargee, and the famous teacher, Yadnyawalkya.

> "'Yadnyawalkya! Since everything in this world is woven, warp and woof, on water, please tell me, on what is water woven, warp and woof?"
>
> Yadnyawalkya said: "Gargee! It is woven on wind."
>
> "On what is wind woven, warp and woof?"
>
> "On the region of the celestial choir."
>
> "On what is the region of the celestial choir woven, warp and woof?"
>
> "On the Sun."
>
> "On what is the Sun woven, warp and woof?"
>
> "On the Moon."

"On what is the Moon woven, warp and woof?"

"On the stars."

"On what are the stars woven, warp and woof?"

"On the region of the gods."

"On what is the region of the gods woven, warp and woof?"

"On the region of light."

"On what is the region of light woven, warp and woof?"

"On the region of the Creator."

"On what is the region of the Creator woven, warp and woof?"

"On the region of Spirit."

"On what is the region of Spirit woven, warp and woof?"

Yadnyawalkya said: "Gargee! Do not transgress the limit; or you may go crazy."

Gargee became silent.'

(pp. 139–40)

Self as infinite

The transcendence of *Brahman* can be explained rationally with reference to the type of argument that Kant used in his three antinomies of pure reason (see *Critique of Pure Reason*, pp. 473–79). We are led by reason, on the one hand, to believe in an infinite chain of causes and effects in space and time, which are the subject matter of natural science. Yet reason also prompts us to believe in some starting point, some first cause, in order to complete the chain, since without this the creation is not an intelligible whole and complete phenomenon. These beliefs contradict one another; neither can be freed from the entanglement of the other. Only by positing a first cause outside or beyond the phenomenal creation can we reconcile the two. Such a transcendental supreme being would be at the origin or source of the infinite chain of causes and effects, not merely antecedent to it in time, and would bring the infinite series to completion in a whole contained within it. Vedanta, indeed, does assert the infinity in time and space of the creation, whilst maintaining that, since it is phenomenal, it is contained within the transcendent *Brahman.*

If *Brahman* itself is not in time, or in any way subject to time, it must be eternal. Clearly this does not mean that it goes on forever, for that would be to give it temporal attributes. Sometimes Vedanta refers to *Brahman* as the ever-present moment, the 'now' which never passes; sometimes it is said to contain the past, present and future. Often it is described as unchanging and unmoving, though not in the sense of an inert object.

> 'It is unmoving, one, and faster than the mind. The senses could not overtake It, since It ran ahead. Remaining stationary, It outruns all other runners.'
>
> (*Eesha* Upanishad, v. 4,
> in *The Ten Principal Upanishads*, p. 9)

Brahman alone is indestructible. As it has no parts and no attributes, it cannot be destroyed by the decay or removal of them. Its nature is existence itself, and existence cannot cease to be. This eternality is also sometimes considered to be identical with the third feature of the nature of *Brahman* (after existence – *sat* –

and consciousness – *chit*) namely bliss or *ananda*. However, lest the positive identification of *Brahman*, or the universal self, as *sat–chit–ananda* induces the student of Vedanta to think that he now knows about the nature of *Brahman*, Sankara gives a warning.

> 'The Absolute [*Brahman*] is that in which there is no particularity. There is no name, no form, no action, no distinction, no genus, no quality. It is through these determinations alone that speech pro-ceeds, and not one of them belongs to the Absolute. So the latter cannot by taught by sentences of the pattern "This is so-and-so." In such Upanishadic phrases and words as "The Absolute is Consciousness-Bliss" [etc] the Absolute is artificially referred to with the help of superimposed name, form and action, and spoken of in exactly the way we refer to objects of perception, as when we say "That white cow with horns is twitching." But if the desire is to express the true nature of the Absolute, void of all external adjuncts and particularity, then it cannot be described by any positive means whatever . . . Whoever wishes to characterize the nature of the Self in this way is like one wishing to roll up the sky like a piece of leather and climb up on it as if it were a step. He is like one hoping to find the tracks of fish in the water or of birds in the sky.'
>
> (*Samkara on the Absolute*, Vol. I of
> *Samkara Sourcebook*, pp. 146–8)

Hence even the statements about the *Brahman* in the Upanishads are no more than directions. They are not knowledge. That is only to be found in the total recognition by the student that he or she is *Brahman*, that there is not one iota of difference between the individual self and the universal self.

The realization of unity

> 'Two birds that are ever associated and have similar names,
> cling to the same tree. Of these, the one eats the fruit of
> divergent tastes, and the other looks on without eating.'
> (*Mandukya* Upanishad, III iI, in *The Eight Upanishads*, p. 143)

What are these two birds? One is the individual self (*Atman* or
jiva), the other is the universal self (*Brahman*). The former
indulges in the fruits of the world by following its desires. It
consumes what it perceives; it follows the senses where they lead;
it takes pleasure in the world. Pleasure and pain attract and repel
it; they colour its experience. In short, it is the experiencer
(*samsarin*), living in and of the world, symbolized by the tree in
which it sits, turning about and pecking at the 'fruit of
divergent tastes'.

The second bird does not move. It merely watches, serene
and untroubled, aware of but not drawn by the delights of the
tree, nor concerned with its snares. The two birds appear to have
different, though similar, names – individual self and universal self
– yet they are also referred to by the very same name 'I'. For there
are not really two birds at all. The pecking bird is a kind of illusion, as is the tree in which it sits. So long as this bird continues
to move and peck, the illusion is maintained. Experience
(*samsara*) of the world as something that exists in its own right,
to be enjoyed by an experiencer, never ceases whilst the bird is
deluded by ignorance. Yet knowledge releases it from the illusory
world. Then it becomes one with its true nature, as a witness
devoid of action and desire. One bird, without a second,
remains, seeing the tree – as before – as no more than an
insubstantial dream.

How many selves in a room?

How are we to relate this analogy to the human situation? Let us
take a more mundane scenario. A man sits in a room full of people.

His experience of what is there is different from that of others. His position in the room is unique; no one else sits where he sits. Therefore what he sees, hears, touches and so on has particular qualities, different from those of others. They may all see the same furniture, for example, but he sees it from a particular angle and height. They may hear the same voices, but he hears them with different degrees of volume and acuteness. Moreover, his attitudes, thoughts and feelings are special to him. He likes someone whom others may dislike and vice versa. Such a catalogue of differences is almost limitless. Therefore, he might conclude, 'I myself have a unique experience; no one else sees what I see.' And, of course, he is right. How can this be denied?

Yet there is one further crucial step which he may unwittingly take. He may conclude that he himself is different from the others in the room, on the grounds that his experience is different. Indeed, he almost certainly began with that as an assumption, and did not need any more experience to convince him of it. 'I am me', he might think, though that would be merely a tautology. How are we to show him that he is mistaken? For the Vedantist, this is the one cardinal mistake, the mother of all mistakes. If we tell the man the story of the two birds, he may simply not recognize it as in any way applicable to him. 'Are you suggesting I am schizophrenic?' he may indignantly ask.

Let us analyze his situation further: all the qualities mentioned above – such as aspects of the furniture, and sounds of voices – are objects of his perception. He is aware of them as objects. So, too, his attitudes, thoughts and feelings are within the field of an inner awareness, if he chooses to pay attention to them – and perhaps even if he does not. What else can he possibly recognize in his situation which is not such an object of awareness? Only one thing – the observing self, the witness. That alone cannot be an object. How then can he possibly identify any quality in that observer which distinguishes it – him – from any 'other' observer in the room? If there appear to be other observers – the people there – then he cannot experience any quality that they have as observers, as opposed to as bodies and minds, which would be different from any qualities that 'his' observer has. There are no such qualities, simply because qualities are observable phenomena, and an observer is unobservable.

If there are putatively several things between which no difference of any kind whatsoever can be found, then it follows that they are the same (identical) thing. Of course, the man might say, 'How ridiculous! The other people are over there and I am here', rather like Dr Johnson refuting Berkeley's idealism by kicking a stone. But the point is that the criteria for saying that they are 'over there' are entirely physical and (perhaps) mental. Bodily characteristics, such as a person's face, and mental ones, such as what she talks about or what feelings she appears to have, enable us to say that the person over there is so-and-so. (We name her.) These are not qualities of the self. There are certainly many people in the room, but we have no good reason for saying that there are many selves.

One further aspect of this example might be considered. The man of common sense might claim that his particular viewpoint on the room must be determined by the fact that his self as an observer observes from a particular point in space and time. If it did not, he might say, then he would have a different viewpoint, a different perspective on the room. Therefore there must be many observers in the room, each with a unique space–time viewpoint. What actually determines the 'view' that he gets is the precise location of his eyes, ears and other sense organs, and indeed of his brain as a physical entity connected to those organs. If these move to another point in the room, his 'view' of the room changes. Again we may conclude that this is no reason for saying that his self is located at one point only and that it moves with his brain and other organs. It no more moves than does the space 'inside' his body. Vedanta draws a positive conclusion from this kind of argument: namely that the self is everywhere in the room, seeing through all eyes, hearing through all ears, as the Upanishads often repeat.

'He is never seen, but is the Witness; He is never heard, but is the Hearer; He is never thought, but is the Thinker; He is never known, but is the Knower. There is no other witness but Him, no other hearer but Him. He is the Internal Ruler, your own immortal self.'

(*Brihadaranyaka* Upanishad, pp. 354–5)

Hence the ultimate observer or witness is totally undifferentiated. The *Brihad* says, 'There is no difference whatsoever in it' (IV iv19). Therefore the witnessing self is one. Such a conclusion cuts across all our usual ways of thinking. It means shutting our eyes to our habitual images of life. But as Wittgenstein said, when accused of shutting his eyes to the possibility of doubt – 'They are shut'.

The analogy of a jar
Approaching this question again, using the analogy, familiar in the Upanishads, between the self and space, a jar limits what is contained within it. Space, however, is not contained within it. Indeed the one space contains the jar. Yet if we can make sense of the odd notion of space in the jar having a mind of its own, it might surely think, 'I am small, limited, of a defined shape.' It might regard space outside the jar – if it knew of it at all – as immensely larger, or as made up of a huge number of little spaces like itself. Of course, if the jar were broken it might, rather abruptly, realize its error, but whilst the jar exists its delusion is maintained.

What, for a human being, is equivalent to the jar? The word *upadhi* is used in Vedanta to mean 'limiting adjuncts'. A person's limiting adjuncts give a false view of the self. They include all the features of body and mind, including location in time and space, causal relations, like parentage, and all the qualities that make the person – for practical purposes – distinctive. Thus good qualities, such as virtues, bad qualities, such as vices, genuine qualities, such as skills, and imaginary qualities, such as delusions about one's ability, are all *upadhis*. In so far as they all induce the person to

say, 'I am so-and-so', they comprise a false picture in his mind of
what he is in reality. Believing himself to be good or bad, he ascribes
qualities to the self which it does not really possess. This is utterly
comprehensive. Even 'I am a student of Vedanta' – or worse, 'I am
a teacher of Vedanta' – are equally *upadhis*. It follows that the
whole work of one who seeks realization is to be free from these
limiting adjuncts.

Other analogies

Many analogies more poetic than jugs are used by the Upanishads
to convey this central but elusive truth of Vedanta, that in reality
there is only one self, that the individual and universal are one, or
'I am *Brahman*'. *Brahman* is the ocean; individuals are waves,
with apparent qualities of their own, but in reality they are only
ocean. Or *Brahman* is the Sun, and individuals are the rays of the
Sun. The rays seem to emerge from the Sun as things distinct from
it, yet how can they be anything but Sun? Where does the Sun
end and sunlight begin? Between the individuals there are differences, and even between the experiencer – the seeking bird in
the tree – and what is experienced – the fruit it eats – there are
differences, yet all are *Brahman*.

> 'Thus though foam, ripple, wave, bubble, etc, which are
> different modifications of the sea, consisting of water,
> are non-different from the sea, still amongst themselves are
> perceived actions and reactions in the form of separating
> or coalescing. And yet the foam, wave, etc, do not lose
> their individuality in relation to one another, even though
> they are modifications of the sea and non-different from
> it, which is but water.'
>
> (*Brahma Sutra Bhasya*, p. 325)

Commenting on a verse in the *Gita*, Sankara uses the analogy of
the Sun in another way. Individuals are like reflected images of the
Sun in water, which may shake and shimmer, whilst the Sun itself

is unmoved. When the water has gone they disappear, whilst the Sun remains. 'Ah,' says the sceptic, 'in that case individuals cease to exist when they die; their lives are bounded by birth and death. What use to them is an eternal self (Sun)?' But the analogy does not break down at that point. Are not the reflections of the Sun made of the light of the Sun? Its light is one, not many. Individuals are manifestations of one self, as a reflection of the Sun manifests sunlight. Hence the eternity of the one self subsumes within it the eternity of the 'individual' selves, as the time-span of the Sun subsumes the time-span of its rays.

I and the world

The doctrine of the identity of the individual self with the self of all others, though contrary to everyday belief, may be acceptable to those who have some sense of a community of spirit, or even just of a common humanity. *Advaita* Vedanta, however, goes much further than this. It denies not only the duality of 'I' and 'you', or 'I' and 'he/she', but also the duality of 'I' and the world. In other words, it is not that conscious beings (or at least human ones) are regarded as essentially one vis-à-vis a separate unconscious world of material things; it is that everything, conscious or otherwise, is regarded as one. All is one. 'All this verily is *Brahman*', declares the *Chandogya* Upanishad. How is this doctrine of an absolute unity to be supported?

Vedanta claims that the truth needs no support. In some scriptures this absolute unity is stated as a fact which should not be questioned. To the Western mind such an approach may sound like sheer dogmatism. Yet Kant, in particular, used a kind of transcendental argument not unlike this method of Vedanta. If a philosophical assumption is made from which arguments and statements can be developed – not necessarily all deductive ones – which themselves deal satisfactorily with many, if not all, of the problems of ontology, epistemology, moral philosophy and so on, then that in itself justifies the original assumption. For a Christian, for example, assuming the existence of Christ as a Man/God solves many problems about the nature of mankind – sin, redemption, free will and so on – which would be otherwise irresolvable. Similarly, the assumption of an absolute unity may provide a solution to questions about substance, matter, mind/body relations, consciousness, life and death and many other questions which prove intractable to dualistic and other standpoints.

Yet teachers in the tradition of *Advaita* have not been so uncompromising as to exclude all discussion of this foundation principle. Indeed the Upanishads themselves offer aids to its acceptance. 'Since the import of the entire scriptures is being summarised here, it is necessary to make the implied meaning explicit', writes Sankara, as a comment on the following verse.

> 'As from a fire kindled with wet faggot diverse kinds of smoke issue, even so, my dear, the Rig Veda, Yajur Veda, Sama Veda, Atharvangirasa, history, mythology, arts, Upanishads, pithy verses, aphorisms, elucidations, explanations, sacrifices, oblations in the fire, food, drink, this world, the next world and all beings are all [like] the breath of this infinite Reality. They are [like] the breath of this [Supreme Self].'
>
> (*Brihadaranyaka* Upanishad, p. 541)

Or, in another verse, this one all-inclusive *Brahman* is like the sound of a drum, when one cannot distinguish the individual beats, for 'they are included in the general note of the drum'. Each stroke is a particular existing thing – a material object, sense impression, thought, emotion, word, human being, separate self – all swallowed up in the one reality of the unbroken roll of a drum.

Sankara's argument from existence

In his *Gita* commentary, Sankara presents an argument, rather than an analogy. *Brahman* is *sat*, or existence, and therefore supports all, for everything is based on existence. 'Everywhere the idea of *sat* is present.' Not even mirages exist without a basis, since they exist as mirages, if not as the things which they appear to be. The water of a mirage of an oasis in the desert cannot quench the thirst or wet the sand, yet as a mirage of an oasis it exists. Kant dismissed the ontological argument, used by Anselm and Descartes to prove the existence of God, with the incisive rebuttal that existence is not a predicate. Sankara's case, however, does not rest on the use of existence as a predicate. His argument is not that, if one tries to strip away all predicates from things which exist, the only one that cannot be removed is existence. It is rather that in so far as our experience contains things at all, whatever their ontological status as real or imagined or illusory or mistaken, they are something, they exist as something, be it a real thing, an image, an illusion or a mistake. What or how they are requires the use of predicates. That they are does not. In short, Sankara would agree with Kant that existence is indeed not a predicate.

Sankara goes on to argue that since in our experience something exists, be it real, illusory or whatever, then the substratum of that is existence itself. He denies that it is possible for anything which is merely an appearance or illusion to exist without a substratum. In the dark a rope may be taken to be a snake. It appears as a snake. But there could not be such an appearance of a snake unless there was a rope to appear so. Similarly, if the whole world is an appearance, then there must be some substratum which is really there, appearing as the world. This substratum is existence itself. The snake exists as an appearance. Existence is *sat*, which is *Brahman*.

What if nothing whatsoever exists? That cannot be so, says Vedanta. Things appear to exist, and to do even that they require the substratum of existence. Existence is the undeniable basis of whatever is, albeit that it is all an illusion. 'This [self] was indeed *Brahman* in the beginning', says the *Brihad*. No thing of any kind whatsoever can come out of nothing or a void. Nor can it be present now without a substratum of being. Many people, including Ludwig Wittgenstein, have had the experience of wondering at the very existence of the world, rather than how it is, or what form it takes. Interestingly enough Wittgenstein related this to the feeling of being absolutely safe. (See *Ludwig Wittgenstein: A Memoir*, p. 70)

'That thou art'

The reason that we do not know that all is *Brahman*, including ourselves, is that ignorance (*avidya*) stands in the way.

> 'Ignorance superimposes on him the idea that he is not *Brahman* and not all, as a mother-of-pearl is mistaken for silver, or as the sky is imagined to be concave, or blue, or the like.'
>
> (*Brihadaranyaka* Upanishad, I v10,
> Sankara commentary, p. 102)

Once more we are confronted with the question of how such ignorance is to be removed. In his *Vakyavritti*, Sankara adopts a method of analysis to dispel the false ideas of duality. He selects for analysis the axiom of identity 'That Thou art' (*Tattvamasi*), one of the four great central aphorisms of Vedanta. What does this cryptic sutra mean? Without any analysis it is simply false. The demonstrative 'That' refers to something presented to the person addressed by the pronoun 'Thou' which is clearly separate from him or her. Hence Sankara has recourse to a semantic distinction. He says that both 'That' and 'Thou' have direct and indirect meanings. The direct meanings are commonsense ones: 'That' means the world as it appears to us, an objective world in space and time, made up of physical things and mental and emotional phenomena. It is all that we are aware of in our experience. The direct meaning of 'Thou' is the person addressed, including all personal characteristics. In other words, it is the usual sense of the second person pronoun when used to stand for a proper name, with all its associated connotations. Thus when the teacher addresses the student he refers to a person of a certain age, physical type, character and so on.

What then are the indirect meanings? A simple and correct

answer to this is to say that they are what the words refer to in reality. Reference is being made to what 'That' and 'Thou' really are. Hence 'That' has the indirect meaning of the substratum of the world, existence itself devoid of all attributes, even of space and time. It is the *Brahman*, pure spirit, of the nature of *sat*, *chit* and *ananda* – being, knowledge (or consciousness) and bliss. Similarly, 'Thou' refers indirectly to the self of the person, the witness within, unmoving, unborn, undying, the *Atman* or immortal soul.

Hence the statement, 'That Thou art', given its indirect meanings, has the same sense as another of the 'great aphorisms' of Vedanta, namely 'This *Atman* is *Brahman*' (*Ayam Atma Brahma*). The individual self is the universal self. To understand, or realize, this truth in the depths of one's being is the end of Vedanta. One who does so is free from the disease of existence in the world; he has passed beyond all personal desires and attachments; he has fulfilled all the duties that his nature and place in society demand of him.

On a merely intellectual level we may trace the form of Sankara's semantic argument by means of an analogy. There was a time when men believed that the Morning Star and the Evening Star were two different stars. Then it was discovered that they were, in fact, one and the same, namely the planet Venus. What then of the sentence 'The Morning Star is the Evening Star.'? This is an identity statement, and indeed it was one even when men believed that there were two separate stars, though they would have said wrongly that the statement was false. The direct meaning of each expression is, on the one hand, a bright light in the sky seen at dusk, which is a star, and, on the other hand, a bright light in the sky seen at dawn, which is a star. The indirect meaning, or what we might call the reference(s) of the two expressions, is in each case just one and the same star (which happens to be a planet!). Astronomers, using various techniques of observation and mathematics, convinced the ignorant public that the direct meanings mainly described inessential aspects of the phenomena. Such

aspects were derived from the spatial and temporal conditions of
the observers, such as standing by the Nile at six o'clock in the
morning. The essential feature was found scientifically by
abstracting from such particular conditions. Stripped of inessential meaning, the indirect meaning remained in both cases 'a star',
and the astronomers showed indeed that it was the same one.
'The Morning Star is the Evening Star.'

The semantics of the statement 'That Thou art' are obvious
enough. However, such elucidation does little to remove the doubt
that besets the student of Vedanta concerning the real identity of
the individual self and the universal self. Sankara is speaking to
those who are prepared to undergo more than a process of intellectual argument. The aspirant must be ready to strip away not
merely meanings of words but attachments to the world and to
his own desires. He must penetrate the appearance of the world,
to move beyond its gross and subtle elements to its inner nature,
to see through the names and forms of things to the one reality
that underlies them all. And he must also look within himself and
penetrate the experiences with which he is identified, which he
calls 'himself' – his thoughts, attitudes, standpoints, emotional
hang-ups – to discover his one unchanging substance. Then he
will realize that these two are in truth one. The outer reality seen
truly is the inner reality seen truly.

Self as universal
Since this book does not aim to offer the reader a method of
meditation, or the face to face guidance of a guru, as a means
to achieve such a realization, it will be useful to resort once more
to the Platonic reasoning used earlier about universals. The
untrained mind thinks that the universal self is enormously
greater than the individual self. Is not the former the 'soul' of
the whole universe and the latter the soul of one individual
human being? Surely – at best – one is a mere tiny part of the
other? But the self is not a particular thing, a kind of atomistic
spirit lurking in the depths of the person. Nor is the 'world soul'

a kind of vast ethereal, animistic vapour pervading everything in space, of which the individual soul is a minute portion. In Plato's sense of universal, the individual self is a universal. The white snowflake is a part of snow, but the whiteness of the snowflake is not a part of whiteness. For whiteness is a universal; it has no parts, though it may have instances. The individual person is a part of the human race, but the individual self is not a part of a universal self; though it is an instance of it. It is as truly and completely the self as the self of all is the self, for they are the same.

The Vedantic concept of the self, especially in the teaching of *Advaita*, is a far cry both from our commonsense view of ourselves as independent conscious human beings, and from that of the modern Western tradition of philosophical enquiry, which analyzes the individual into a separate mind/body entity. Yet it need not be regarded as an esoteric or alien concept. We may recall what a master of *Advaita*, Ramana Maharshi, said to a student.

> 'Is there any moment when Self is not? It is not new. Be as you are.'
>
> *(Talks*, p. 46)

Ego

Freud regarded the ego as the executive function of personality. This is rather close to the Vedantic concept of *ahankara*, usually translated as 'ego'. *Ahan* means 'I' (and also 'I am'), whilst *kara* means 'doer', 'maker' or 'author'. The compound Sanskrit word *ahankara* thus means 'I (am) the doer' or 'I as an executive function'. How then is this related to the idea that the real self is the *Brahman*, the universal spirit present in everyone and everything?

Brahman does nothing. It is witness, observer and source of all, yet itself does not act. Actions take place in *maya*, the dream of *Brahman* constituting the world (*see* pp. 118–20). Nature alone moves events to unfold in the form of human actions and other occurrences. People, however, think that they are the original cause

of action, that they do things. We hold within us the root thought
or idea that 'I am the doer'. In truth, as the Upanishads repeat, 'I
do nothing at all'. Where does this leave the ego, the doer, maker
and author?

Surprisingly it leaves ego close to where Freud located it. Ego,
he claimed, is a kind of mediator between the unconscious and
the conscious realms. It helps to integrate the inner and the outer.
Vedanta sees the ego as similarly placed, with one vital difference
– namely the falsity of ego. Ego is the root of all thinking, a kind
of master 'I-thought' from which stem thoughts about the world
and one's role in it. This, however, is not evidence of its real
potency, but of the contrary, as a conversation between Ramana
Maharshi and a student makes clear:

> *RM*: The mind is only a bundle of thoughts. The thoughts
> have their root in the 'I-thought'. Whoever investigates
> the origin of the 'I-thought', for him the ego perishes. This
> is the true investigation. The true 'I' is then found shining
> by itself.

> *Student*: This 'I-thought' arises from me. But I do not know
> the Self.

> *RM*: All these are only mental concepts. You are now iden-
> tifying yourself with a wrong 'I', which is the 'I-thought'.
> This 'I-thought' rises and sinks, whereas the true signifi-
> cance of 'I' is beyond both. There cannot be a break in
> your being. There was no 'I-thought' in your sleep, whereas
> it is present now. The true 'I' is not apparent and the false
> 'I' is parading itself. This false 'I' is the obstacle to your
> right knowledge. Find out where-from this false 'I' arises.
> Then it will disappear. You will be only what you are – i.e.
> absolute Being.

> (*Talks*, p. 192)

According to Sankara in his *Gita* commentary (p. 209), this falsity of the ego is derived from ignorance lodged deep within the mind as a 'latent unconscious impression of *ahankara*'. The dualistic belief in an individual self, separate and independent of the real self, secretes itself there and creates the idea of an agent or doer.

Burdened with the concept of ego, people undertake to do, to make, to authorize, to be responsible for their actions. They see themselves as agents in the world. Ego is the point of reference in this world. Whatever they perceive, enjoy or suffer is referred to this false self. It governs their lives, for egoism is the 'impelling cause of all' (*Gita* commentary, p. 209). As the *Oxford Dictionary of English* defines it, ego is a person's sense of self-esteem or self-importance; and indeed these are fulfilled by the seeming ability to do. What would happen to our self-esteem if we realized that we do nothing whatsoever? But, as Ramana Maharshi asks, how important is this sense of I when we are asleep?

> 'The same one who is now speaking was in deep sleep also. What is the difference between these two states? There are objects and play of senses now which were not in sleep. A new entity, the ego, has risen up in the meantime, it plays through the senses, sees the objects, confounds itself with the body and says that the Self is the ego. In reality, what was in deep sleep continues to exist now too. The Self is changeless. It is the ego that has come between. That which rises and sets is the ego; that which remains changeless is the Self.'
>
> (*Talks*, p. 129)

People sometimes experience a loss of ego even when awake. Under the influence of a shock or crisis, or perhaps for no apparent reason at all, there is a feeling of no one being present, of a kind of void, of not knowing who or what one is. Such an experience can sometimes be terrifying. Does Vedanta lead to this state of metaphysical limbo? Fortunately not, for while it denies the reality of the ego, it asserts the absolute reality of the real self, the *Atman* or *Brahman*. No one is ever really in a void, without a self, howsoever they may believe this. A master of Vedanta knows that the ego is unreal, a false 'I-thought', but as a person in the world he continues to act, to do things like anyone else. The difference is that he does not believe that he himself really does them. He knows that he is the witness of what 'he does'. His own actions are just like the actions of others – movements in nature, events in the 'field' – whilst he is the observer of the field. The lower knowledge says, 'I do'; the higher knowledge says, 'I do nothing at all'.

Chapter 4

Consciousness

'To be conscious is not to be in time'

This line that occurs in T.S. Eliot's 'Burnt Norton' not only expresses a poetic insight; it could also be taken as a statement in Vedanta about consciousness. This is certainly not the common understanding. Ordinarily we believe that we are conscious in time, that consciousness, or states of it, come and go with the passing of time, rather like headaches. Moreover, we think that we each possess consciousness as an attribute, even to the extent of calling it 'mine' or 'yours'. 'My consciousness on the morning after the party was clouded', we might say. We think that we are conscious for most of the day and unconscious during most of the night. If someone hits you on the head with a hammer, you 'lose' consciousness. And if you die, you have lost it permanently – although some would believe that you might regain it in heaven or hell. Similarly we believe in degrees of consciousness. As we fall asleep, we feel it slipping away. If we are ill or drunk or drugged, consciousness may seem to ebb and flow.

How many of these well-established beliefs are really justified? There can be few doubts as to the actual occurrence of these kinds of events. The question is whether they are really about consciousness. Should they be more accurately described in some other way? We could say, instead of 'I am losing consciousness', for example, 'Consciousness is losing me'! The concept is notoriously difficult to pin down.

Western philosophers can almost be placed in schools of thought according to their views about it, ranging from outright materialists at one extreme to transcendental idealists at the other. For the former, like Karl Marx, consciousness is an epi-phenomenon, a merely subjective effect in classes of people produced objectively by their relationship to the material means of production in a particular society. For the latter, consciousness in the form of apperception, or inner awareness, is a kind of thread which links experiences together as the objects of a single conscious subject. In between are those who believe consciousness to be a concomitant of brain states, perhaps determined by them, but nevertheless ontologically distinct. Some would regard the word 'consciousness' as simply a means of describing large areas of human behaviour which cannot be adequately described in physical or determinant terms.

Vedanta is radical where consciousness is concerned. It denies all the features put forward above as 'common understanding'. Consciousness is, indeed, as T.S. Eliot wrote, outside of time. It is not possessed by individuals, nor indeed by anything, for it is not an attribute. It does not come and go, however much it may appear to do so. You cannot 'lose' consciousness, even when hit by a sledgehammer. Nor is it lost on death. It does not even have degrees. To believe that it does is like believing that your train is accelerating out of a station, when it is the train on the next platform that is moving the other way. In short, all these so-called features of consciousness are illusory. They belong to the world of appearances and not to reality.

For consciousness is real. It exists independently of all phenomena, like the cinema screen in relation to the play of events on it created by the projector. Like the screen, also, it does not move, change or cease to be there. How can Vedanta justify a view of consciousness so opposed to our normal beliefs? To find the answer we may turn to the classic statement made about consciousness in the *Mandukya* Upanishad.

The argument of the *Mandukya*

In the *Mandukya* we are taken in turn through the three states of waking, dreaming and sleeping. Superficially they appear as conditions of consciousness experienced by an individual and easily recognized by everyone. Waking is described as a state of awareness of external objects seen through the eyes, heard through the ears and so on. This objective world is observed to be in space and includes the physical body, but it is outside the observing individual who experiences it. In short, it is the world in which we ordinarily think we live. By contrast, the dream state is awareness of the inner world of mind, not present in space and recognized by means of 'inner senses', such as seeing, as when we see a tiger in a dream, or imagine one when otherwise awake. The third state, deep, dreamless sleep, contains no objects, neither external nor inner, and consequently has no differentiation of any kind. No desires are experienced in this state, for there is nothing there to be desired. It is blissful and is also called the 'doorway' to the dreaming and waking states.

These states are not states of consciousness, according to the *Mandukya*, but states of the intelligent part of the mind (*buddhi*) (*see* pp. 148–9). For there is a crucial fourth step in the argument, which introduces consciousness, not as a fourth state but as the substratum of all three. It is a seamless backcloth to the play of the three states, which prevents their being unrelated or disparate experiences without a common subject. As 'the essence of the one self-cognition common to all states', it is akin to Kant's concept of the transcendental unity of apperception, which establishes the necessary unity of empirical experience as that of a single subject. Unity is given in the *Mandukya* by a 'something' which is not conscious of the external world, nor of the inner world, nor of both together, and which is not the undifferentiated state of sleep. It is neither conscious, nor unconscious; it is beyond all empirical observation, inaccessible to action, unrelated, inconceivable, uninferable, unimaginable, indescribable. It does not change, and neither has in itself, nor experiences, duality of any kind. That 'something' is pure consciousness.

How then is this consciousness to be known? Nothing can be conscious of it, for if it were there would be an infinite regress of types of consciousness. Therefore there cannot be a knower of it, nor can it be known as an object. Yet it is known from the very fact of its own being. It contains, as it were, its own validation. In each of the three states of waking, dreaming and sleeping, consciousness is present as the fundamental unity which makes them known to itself as knower. In knowing them it necessarily knows itself. What the three states have in common, what is the same in them, is consciousness. Their sameness is consciousness.

There is, however, an overriding error in this account. Throughout the argument the superficial reference to the individual has been assumed. Waking, dreaming and sleeping are taken to be what an individual readily acknowledges as his states, and even the elusive concept of pure consciousness is not hard to relate to one's experience as an individual. 'It is certainly me who was asleep last night, dreamed for a while and am awake now!', each of us might say. 'I am the observer of this particular body and these dreams, and I do not cease to exist when sleeping. I am one – how easy the *Mandukya* is to understand!'

Universal, not individual, self

Such a view can only be sustained by ignoring a great deal of what the *Mandukya* actually says, such as, 'All this is surely *Brahman*. The self is *Brahman*', a categorical assertion of *Advaita*, leaving no room for doubt that the self referred to is the one self of all. And it was this same one self that has the four 'quarters', analyzed further as waking, dreaming and sleeping, plus the fourth 'quarter' containing and underlying the first three. The description of the state of sleep is a further strong clue to the universal nature of the self, for it says, 'This one [sleep] is the source of all . . . the place of origin and dissolution of all beings.' The sleeping state of an individual can hardly be the source and place of dissolution of every being in the universe.

Sankara's commentary also emphasizes that the _Mandukya_ is to be understood in terms of a universal, not an individual, self. He says, for example, of the first 'quarter' that the entire phenomenal universe is comprehended in the waking state, and that the self at issue is not the 'indwelling self, as circumscribed by one's own body.' In other words, the waking state of the universal self is the objective physical universe of perceivable things, of which we as individuals are aware. Similarly, Sankara says that the dream state is the same as universal mind, and quotes the _Svetasvatara_ Upanishad's description of mind as 'one effulgent being hidden in all creatures' (_Svetasvatara_ VI 11). As for the state of sleep, he supports the _Mandukya_ by remarking that it is a state of immanence in all diversity, which gives rise to the universe.

Undoubtedly then the _Mandukya_'s account of the four 'quarters' implicitly and, at times, explicitly rests on a concept of the self which identifies the innermost feature of the individual person with the supreme spirit or _Brahman_. However, the _Mandukya_ is not discussing a universal, impersonal self, devoid of connection with humanity and not recognizable by individual people. On the contrary, since it is written for the aspirant who seeks a true understanding of the nature of things and not for the wise, who already understand, its aim is to make intelligible to the individual the reality of the universal self as being the same as himself. Were this not so the _Mandukya_ would conflict with the aphorism 'That Thou art' and indeed with all other Upanishadic statements of _Advaita_. Hence the self in this context is not exclusively an individual self, nor exclusively a universal self, for it is both. Like the Morning Star and the Evening Star, each can be recognized by its own criteria, though in fact they are the same.

The _Mandukya_ restated

It will be useful to run through the argument of the _Mandukya_ once more from this standpoint. What now is the waking state?

Firstly, we can say that the objective world of objects in space and the individual's perception of such objects are not two states of affairs but one. There is only one world of perceived objects. Each individual, of course, perceives them directly, but that is not a ground for making each individual perception into an entity or existent thing. My sighting of a pot and the presence of a pot are not two cases, each of which has an ontological status of its own. All that exists in the objective world is a pot. I see a particular aspect of it from my body's unique position in space. The aspect is not a thing in my mind – or anywhere else either. There is only one space. Pots are contained in it, and our view of pots in space is not taking place in another space, which we might call 'my space'. As before, we may conclude that *Advaita* definitely does not embrace sense data, or any kind of empirical idealism. Nor is my view of a pot taking place in something called 'my waking state'. The only waking state is the objective world of objects, like pots. Is there then no individual waking state at all? Yes, there is, but it consists simply of my participation in the universal waking state of objects, just as my view of a pot is my participation in the existence in space of a pot. My waking state is not a kind of annexe, separate from the much larger room of an objective world, or universal waking state. It is more like a window into it.

Yet how are we to understand the spatial world of physical objects as a waking state at all? An explanation of this lies in the *Advaita* view that space is one element amongst the eight that collectively are the manifestation of *Brahman* as the created universe. Above space in this hierarchy of elements is the ego, or sense of self, and below it lie the elements, which make up the world of objects seen, touched, tasted and smelled. (Hearing is associated with the element of space itself.) Hence space is not external to our awareness of spatial things, for our awareness as directed through the ego contains space. As Kant would have agreed, space is in us. But, since there is only one space, such a conclusion supports the *Advaita* proposition that 'we' are one consciousness, rather than numerous disparate ones. Space then is a chief feature of a single waking state in which we, as individuals, participate. We are members, as bodies, of one physical world of objects. Our awareness of this in the form of a waking state is no more than participation in one universal waking state, constituted by the physical world of space, which exists within one universal consciousness. When Schiller read Kant's *Transcendental Aesthetic*, which explains how space is 'in us', he exclaimed that it was as though he had walked out of the darkness into a lighted room!

How then are we to understand the dream 'world' as a universal state? Surely this above all is an individual matter? My dreams are uniquely mine. No one else can possibly have access to them, except in so far as I tell others about them. Is there not one dream state associated with each individual? Do we not each have a mind of our own, in which occur dreams, imaginings and other essentially private events? Let us examine, however, the notion of a universal mind, or universal 'dream world'. Phenomena unobservable by direct sense perception, but revealed by science, might constitute this, or what is basically the same thing, the world of entities, forces and laws serving to explain directly observable phenomena. Atoms, sub-atomic particles, nuclear forces, laws of electro-magnetism and so on explain the observable states and movements of the things we perceive around us.

On occasion scientists have become informed about this unobservable 'world' through the dream state. An outstanding example occurred in 1865, when the German chemist, Kekule, had been grappling with the problem of the structure of the benzene molecule. He dreamt of a snake biting its tail while in a whirling motion. From this dream was born the concept of a six-carbon benzene ring, which enabled the known facts of organic chemistry to be unified into a structured system. Moreover, the 'world' of theories, hypotheses and conjectures, combined with the mathematics that these usually require, are very much the product of mental activity, and might be classified themselves as mental phenomena par excellence. Plato certainly seemed to regard them as entities of a superior order to anything perceived by the senses, when he placed them in the lower half of the intellectual world in his analogy of the line. One is reminded of Schrodinger's assertion that all that finally exists for physicists are mathematical equations. For the sake of argument, let us take this 'world' of unobservable phenomena to be the universal mind referred to in the *Mandukya* – or at least a significant part of it. Other quite different areas of human experience might also be contained in it; such as common emotional responses, like empathy.

The difficult philosophical problem that now remains is how to understand the identity of an individual dream state and the universal dream state. Is the former also a kind of window through which we see into the one great dream of the universal mind? Instances of people feeling that they have entered into such a mind, and then returned to the normal condition of their own individual mind, may be helpful, but they do not offer good grounds for the identity, only for the existence of both. For this is not a case of finding evidence of the ability to move from one to the other, but of finding good reasons to believe that these two are in fact one – that the personal mind is the universal mind when seen truly. How is the perfectly ordinary experience of dreaming or imagining to be seen as an action or event in the one mind of all, a universal dream state, analogous to the universal waking state of the one physical world?

Two approaches may be taken to this problem. The first is the negative method of destroying belief in a private world of mental objects. Wittgenstein brought forward a range of arguments on this score. One of them at least illustrates his method. An object is something that can be re-identified, or in other words has a reasonable degree of continuity in time as identically the same object. But how can a mental object, like an imagined pot, be re-identified if it exists in a private world? I may say that I feel sure that my memory of a pot is of the same pot I imagined a few moments ago, but how can I distinguish between being correct and being incorrect? Are there any criteria for saying that the pot has in fact stayed the same or changed? If I say it is the same, does that make it the same? Can I be mistaken? If not, then there is no difference at all between an objective pot and a 'pot' which continually transforms itself into other shapes and colours which I fail to notice. Hence there is no such thing as a pot-object. Nor are there any other private mental objects. This does not mean that such experiences as one person imagining a pot do not occur. It means simply that they do not occur in a private world.

This negative argument is interestingly related to a positive argument derived from the teaching of Sankara. According to *Advaita*, the origin and cause of everything is *Brahman*. This, however, may be understood through language as the syllable *OM*, the sacred word which denotes *Brahman*. 'That very Self, considered from the standpoint of the syllable [denoting it] is *OM*.' (*Mandukya* v. 8). From this primary sound emanate all words. Words in turn create the phenomena which are experienced in mental and physical worlds as things in the dreaming or waking states, since all particular things are really no more than names that give rise to forms. Thus the word for an oak tree – not in any particular language, but as a more fundamental sound – creates an oak tree. It follows that an imagined oak tree is created by the original sound peculiar to it. Yet this sound is not uniquely present in an individual mind. It exists as an emanation from the *Brahman* itself, and it takes its stand in the universal mind to which individuals have access by means of language (*see* pp. 179–82).

Language, as Wittgenstein demonstrated, is a public and interpersonal activity, not a private one. Words and sentences depend upon correct usage, or rules. If there were no way of distinguishing correct from incorrect usage, there would be no language, as Lewis Carroll so frequently implied. So these negative and positive arguments, by two philosophers greatly removed in time and place, for the ultimate incoherence of the idea of an individual mind are – rather surprisingly – closely related.

What then of the third state of deep sleep? Once more we are faced with an apparent dichotomy between the individual's conviction that his state of sleep belongs uniquely to him and the existence of a universal sleeping state, which is 'the place of origin and dissolution of all beings'. Since the state of dreamless sleep involves no objects and no sense of an observing subject, indeed no obvious duality of any kind, the problem is perhaps less acute than in the case of waking and dreaming. Yet the individual, when he awakes, does have some kind of memory of having been in a state of deep sleep, and also does respond, when in deep sleep, to stimuli such as noise and touch. Are these evidence for an individual state? External stimuli are not themselves contents of the sleep state. They arouse perceptions which are audible and tactile, for example, and therefore occur in the waking or dreaming states; presumably the latter if they are prior to waking. As for the memory of having slept, that also has no content if the sleep was dreamless, and *a fortiori* has no content in an individual state. It could just as well be understood as the memory of a universal state. It is not unreasonable to say that all individuals 'go to the same place' when they sleep.

What, however, is this universal 'place' of sleep? Shakespeare hints at its universality:

> 'Balm of hurt minds, great nature's second course,
> Chief nourisher in life's feast.'
>
> (*Macbeth* II 2)

Science, too, is perhaps not averse to the idea of a single, common origin of all created things; a kind of matrix containing in potential the forms of everything. As Plato wrote:

> 'The original of the universe contains in itself all intelligible beings,
> just as this world comprehends us and all other visible creatures.'
>
> (*Timaeus*, 30)

The *Mandukya* leaves no doubt about the universal nature of the state of sleep, for it describes it as the Lord of all, omniscient and the inner director of all (v. 6). Many people have the experience of discovering some new knowledge in relation to a question they have 'slept on'. Since – if it is new – it is not, by definition, something they are merely recalling from a personal store of knowledge, then it might owe its origin to a universal store, the potential of everything created. Combined with the negative reason that no experiential content can be given to an individual state of sleep, these hints at the existence of a universal state may be sufficient, at least, to weaken our belief in the former. This does not eliminate the commonsense view that a single person may be asleep. What it does is to re-interpret this as a case of an individual partaking in the universal state of sleep, which is ever-present as the world in potential. Indeed, if the world manifested as created things really arises from such a potential, why should not individuals, such as artists, find their inspiration by entering into it? The process of artistic creation is not unlike the refreshment of the body and mind in sleep.

Consciousness is not a state
None of these states, individual or universal, are consciousness. They are simply states of intelligence (*buddhi*). Consciousness itself is the one, undifferentiated, ever constant, self-validating, self-conscious presence in all three states. It is the witness of whatever state the intelligence undergoes. And lest the idea of a witness is taken to imply a duality between a witnessing subject and witnessed objects, the *Mandukya* reminds us that the whole phenomenal world represented by the three states is in reality negated when the truth about pure consciousness is realized. For this is the 'limit of the negation of the phenomenal world'. (v. 12) In other words, when consciousness is found to be the sole reality, the phenomenal world is known to be unreal. Hence nothing, in truth, is witnessed by consciousness. It is unmixed with experience.

This idea that consciousness has no object, but exists alone as the one reality, may be easier to comprehend if we remember that consciousness itself is not conscious. Nor is it unconscious. For any universal, like whiteness, logically cannot partake of itself as a quality. Whiteness is not white. If it were then there would have to be another whiteness which lends itself to the first one, and so on. A concept which requires infinite regression is unintelligible. But if consciousness is not conscious, then it is not conscious of anything. It is merely awareness, knowledge, witness – without an object. It may appear to witness the three states, but even that is an aspect of the illusion. When the rope appears to be a snake, how can the 'snake' be witnessed, for there is no snake?

The nature of consciousness

What cannot be known as an object, nor recognized as a subject, is beyond the grasp of exact language. Yet since, according to Vedanta, we are in essence nothing but consciousness, it cannot in reality be in any sense remote or obscure. The analogy of light perhaps come closest to explaining it.

> 'Have no doubt about the fact that you are not other than the consciousness which is the self illuminating the modifications of the mind.'
>
> (*Vakyavritti of Sri Sankaracharya*, v. 21 p. 13)

The dream state shows how the analogy of light is accurate, and yet only an analogy. In a dream, or a process of imagination, we experience things or events much as they are in the 'real' world. We see them in the mind. But there is no actual light in the dream world. So what is the 'light' by which we see things there? One might say that imagined light is there, like imagined pots or whatever. But in what does the imagined light with its illumined objects occur? What lights up – as it were – our imagination? What enables us to see, and indeed to hear, touch and so on, in the imagined or dream world? That is consciousness, the 'light' which enables dream perception to occur at all. For who dreams and imagines?

Is it not a conscious self that does so? The dream takes place in that consciousness. There is nothing else in which it could occur.

In the *Brihadaranyaka* Upanishad, the sage Yadnyawalkya explains how the conscious self is like light. 'The Sun is the light of man' is his first proposition. But what if the Sun has set? Then the Moon is the light of man. What if there is no Moon? Then fire is the light of man. What if fire is out? Then speech is the light of man, for even when a man cannot see he can hear a voice. What if nothing is said? Then, 'Self is his light; by that light man sits, works, goes, returns'.

The ever-present nature of consciousness is most starkly demonstrated in the case of deep sleep, the very condition in which we ordinarily think of ourselves as totally unconscious. Sankara examines this, when a student of *Advaita* says:

> *Student*: 'But I have never experienced anything in dreamless sleep, whether consciousness or anything else.'
>
> *Sankara*: 'And yet you *do* have experience in dreamless sleep, because you deny that you have experienced anything, while not denying the fact of experiencing. I told you before that that experience of yours was itself consciousness. That which is present and enables you to make the denial "I did not experience anything", that is your experience, your knowledge. Therefore, since the light of consciousness never fails in waking, dream or dreamless sleep it is self-established as eternal and constant and raised above all change, and it does not depend on being established by empirical means of proof.'
>
> (*Samkara on the Absolute*, pp. 213–14)

The Kantian idea of the necessary unity of experience is applicable here. Something enables the condition of deep sleep to be brought within the unity of experience of a single self. We would never want to say that when we slept, someone or something else was sleeping. I, who say that I slept, was the one who slept, not another. How do I know this? Wittgenstein might argue that this is not the kind of thing that is known, just as I do not know my own pain – I just have it. But it does not really matter if we leave out knowing that it was I who slept. We can just as well say that it makes no sense for one person to say that he slept and another person or thing to have been the sleeper concerned. It is simply a truth requiring no support or reason that he who speaks of sleeping was he who slept. Experience is unintelligible if it is not the experience of one conscious self.

The idea, however, that we are unconscious in dreamless sleep is deeply rooted. For one thing, it matches the Freudian concept of the unconscious being beyond the ego. If the ego stands between the conscious and the unconscious, then surely it is the waking state of awareness of an external world that is conscious, and the 'hidden' world 'behind' the ego that is unconscious? Not at all, says Ramana Maharshi. 'That which lies beyond the ego is consciousness.' (*Talks*, p. 81). Consciousness is not what it appears to be. Since it is most clearly present in sense perception, in our most obvious feelings, like pain and pleasure, and in our transient emotions, like affection, hatred and anger, we do not notice how it is really distinct from them. It appears so mixed with these experiences that we forget that it is equally present in dreams and in the seemingly unconscious state of sleep.

The eye of the eye

This presence of consciousness 'within' sense perception is examined closely by Sankara in his commentary on the *Brihadaranyaka* Upanishad (III iv 2), where he analyzes 'seeing' into two components. One is a function of the mind, which connects with the eye and is an act with a beginning and an end. The second is 'the witness of vision', which has neither beginning nor end, for it is eternal. 'The vision of the witness can never be lost.' (*Brihadaranyaka* IV iii 23). It is the eye of the eye, the ear of the ear, reminiscent of the Psalmist, who asked:

'He that planted the ear, shall he not hear? He that formed the eye, shall he not see?

(Psalm 94)

Modern philosophers, such as Gilbert Ryle, have subjected this idea – that the function of seeing is itself seen – to much scrutiny, usually with the conclusion that it is nonsensical, since it creates an infinite regress. If seeing requires a further, more interior, seeing, then does not this second seeing require another seeing *ad infinitum*? But this rhetorical question, in fact, has the answer 'No'. The second seeing is not the same kind of seeing as the first. Seeing with the mind and eye is one thing (which admittedly has philosophical problems of its own); seeing by the witness is another. The act of seeing has a witness, which is consciousness. That is not an act, for it is not a temporal phenomenon. It is, as Kant might have said, noumenal. It is the constant, ever-present ground that alone makes sense perception, and all our experience, possible; the one consciousness that is everyone's secret. 'To be conscious is not to be in time.'

Chapter 5

Liberation

Action

The Vedantic maxim 'I do nothing at all' is central to the whole system of *Advaita* Vedanta, and yet to the Western mind it is a complete paradox. On the one hand, it is said that he who truly appreciates it is fully realized. On the other hand, it seems to be self-stultifying. How can the highest development of a human being, the culmination of man's intelligence, love and power, be associated with doing nothing, with the complete inability to act?

To find the answer to this paradox, let us begin with a forthright statement of Sankara's, which explicitly denies that the self acts.

> 'The knower of *Brahman* has this realization: "As opposed to the entity known before as possessed of agentship and experiencership [sic] by its very nature, I am *Brahman* which is by nature devoid of agentship and experiencership in all the three periods of time. Even earlier I was never an agent and experiencer, nor am I so at present, nor shall I be so in future."'
>
> (*Brahma Sutra Bhasya*, p. 837)

So the self as *Brahman* is never an agent. It does nothing. It is the self as ego, as the idea that 'I am the doer', that appears to act. How can we come to terms with such a radical view of action?

Ordinarily we see ourselves from two standpoints. We are aware of the world and what it contains as something objective. We believe ourselves to be, as subjects, observers of it, who know, or fail to know, all sorts of things about it. Vedanta concludes that this first standpoint is ultimately false, based upon the dualism of 'me' and the world. *Advaita* asserts the unity of these. All is *Brahman*. But there is a second standpoint, which is also exceedingly habitual – indeed, which is very dear to us – namely that we are agents.

Surely I cannot doubt that I do things? I walk, run, sit, speak, eat and use my hands. These are deliberate actions. Also, I do things such as breathe and digest; not perhaps so obviously actions, since they are not deliberate. Then there are some actions, like those of sexual behaviour, which are perhaps semi-deliberate. In any of these three cases, whenever I regard myself as an agent, I believe myself to be responsible for my actions. But if I do not do them, how can I possibly be responsible? My recognition of guilt and shame, my acceptance of praise and blame, my acknowledgment of the justice of reward and punishment, indeed my whole place in society with its moral code and laws, seem to depend upon the principle that I am responsible for my actions. So how can I live as a normal person in an organized society if I accept the extraordinary idea that I do nothing at all? We will come back to this searching question later (*see* pp. 94–6).

Action in the *Gita*

The *Bhagavad Gita* has much to say about action. Arjuna, the Pandava brother whose dilemma on the battlefield poses the questions that he puts to his divine charioteer, Krishna, is a man of action. His life as a member of the warrior (*kshatriya*) caste turns upon his ability to act decisively. *Kshatriyas* are akin to Plato's guardians in the *Republic*. They are born to rule the State and to protect it from its enemies within and without. They are trained from childhood in the arts of executive government, in following and administering the law, in the martial arts. Their role is intimately bound up with action in society. Lesser men acknowledge their right to rule, and see them as exemplars of the good life, of how to act well. Like Plato's guardians they possess the cardinal virtues of courage, temperance, wisdom and justice. How could a *kshatriya* accept that he does not really act? (*See* pp. 203–7.)

Arjuna and his four brothers have been deprived of their kingdom by the Kaurava family, kinsmen of the Pandavas. They offer to waive most of their rights if they are allowed to continue to rule a few villages, but the Kaurava king, Duryodhana, will not grant them an iota of land. Warfare is the only recourse. When Arjuna turns to his charioteer in despair at the thought of slaughtering his own kinsmen, Krishna begins a discourse which reveals the secret of action. In doing so he convinces Arjuna to act by fighting with all his might against those whom he loves. A fine sense of irony permeates the *Gita*. Its profound doctrine is that one does not act; yet the gist of Krishna's address to Arjuna is to remove the doubts that inhibit his action! We may sympathize with the bewildered Arjuna when he asks:

> 'You praise renouncing action, and yet praise
> Performance of it too. How is this so?
> Tell me, O Krishna, Lord of all the earth,
> Has action, or inaction, greater worth?'
> (*Bhagavad Gita*, V 1, p. 63)

'Action? Inaction? What in truth are these?' (*Gita*, IV 16). Krishna's answer, as expounded by Sankara, is that actions are performed by the physical body and the mind, not by the self. When the organs of body and mind operate, the ignorant man ascribes their actions to himself. He imagines that he himself acts. 'I am the agent, mine is action, by me shall the fruit of action be reaped.' (*Gita*, Sankara commentary, p. 131.) Whereas the wise man, enlightened as to the real nature of the self, knows that only the apparatus of body and mind act. He sees inaction in action. The inaction of the self is within the action of the organs, like the perfect centre of a wheel within the movement of the spokes and rim. 'The still point of the turning world', as T.S. Eliot puts it ('Burnt Norton', II).

Actions and events

Such an analysis provokes criticism from Western philosophers. There is a fundamental distinction between actions and events. The latter simply happen. They occur in causal relationships. An event has an antecedent cause, or a set of sufficient conditions for its occurrence. (Modern physics may modify this in view of the indeterminacy principle, but this does not affect the argument. Events still happen, if not in the way that Newton and Kant thought.) When the electric light goes on, the wires, the source of current, the bulb, must be in place and the switch moved to the 'on' position. These inanimate things do not act; they have no desires, aims, motives, purposes, responsibilities or intentions. Their part is merely to form links in a causal chain leading to the event. But when I put the light on by moving the switch, I act. I have desires and aims in doing so. My act is intentional.

Another example emphasizes this distinction even more. Two men are sitting in a room, holding a conversation. A group of sturdy ruffians rush into the room and bodily carry out one of the occupants. His companion calls out to him, 'Why are you going?' This was a droll remark precisely because it was inappropriate to suggest that the man had willed, or decided, or intended to leave. His being carried out was an event, not an action, as far as he was concerned. It happened to him; he did not do it.

So if we adopt the Vedantic standpoint that the self is not an agent and does nothing, does this obliterate the vital distinction, making our understanding and language concerning human beings seem hopelessly deficient? If actions involve, in particular, intentional behaviour, does the Vedantist destroy the very notion of action by asserting that it is only the movement of bodily and mental organs?

Intentions

If we look, however, at the concept of intention, is it the self which intends? We certainly think and say that 'I intend to . . .', and also believe that other people may have intentions. Yet this may be just as misleading as in the case of perception. 'I do not really see or hear' says the Vedantist. The eye and mind see, not the self, though the 'inner vision' of the self or knower can never be lost. Just as the self is simply the witness of perceiving, may it not also be simply the witness of action, even including the intentions which actions require?

But can I witness my own intentions? I can certainly witness my own thoughts and desires; why not intentions also? The problem is that intentions are very 'close in'. I may, for example, predict what will happen to me, but can I predict what intentional action I will take? That is surely to make the intention now, not to predict that I will have it in the future. This does not, however, rule out my observing or witnessing my present intentions. Indeed, the fact that I may like or dislike them, and resolve upon them or withdraw them for this reason, shows that, in some sense, I see what they are. I no more have to be identified with my intentions than I have to be identified with any other 'contents' of my mind.

Once again Wittgenstein throws an interesting light on this question by helping to dispel the idea of private worlds in which we each have private things, such as intentions. Such private intentions would be utterly inaccessible to others, except in so far as we say what they are, or others guess what they are by watching our behaviour. In my private world appears my intention, for example, to leave the room. No one else can possibly know this. But I may tell them by saying 'I intend to leave' or they may guess – not know! – when they see that I am getting up from my armchair, or perhaps earlier when the doorbell rings. Wittgenstein challenges this 'picture', as he calls it.

> 'An intention is embedded in its situation, in human customs
> and institutions. If the technique of the game of chess did

> not exist, I could not intend to play a game of chess . . .
> To say "He alone can know what he intends" is nonsense:
> to say "He alone can know what he will do", wrong. For
> the prediction contained in my expression of intention (for
> example "when it strikes five I am going home") need not
> come true, and someone else may know what will
> really happen.'
>
> (*Philosophical Investigations*, pp. 92, 190)

Other people are able to know what someone intends to do,
because the criteria for knowing it are that the action concerned
is, in fact, taking place, and that there are good grounds for claiming
to know. If the doorbell rings, I know that a particular person
intends to answer it, if she gets up and moves towards the door.
It would be a misuse of language to say that I only guessed it.
Hence the picture of a private world in which intentions figure
prominently is false. Since most intentional actions take place in
a 'public' world, this is not surprising.

What bearing does this brief excursion into the concept of
intention have on our understanding of Vedanta? A great deal, for
it makes it rather easier to accept that the self does not act. If acts
are (usually) intentional, then if the intention is knowable by ordinary criteria – like how a person moves or what event actually
happens – then there is not an agent who uniquely knows what
he himself intends. In other words, there is no private self who
intends whenever an intentional act is performed. This conclusion
at least leaves room for a self which does not do anything, and
therefore *a fortiori* does not intend. Intentional acts may be
witnessed by the self, without being intended by the self.
They are intended by the ego performing the function of an agent
(*see* pp. 65–8).

A final comment on the problem of intentions: the Sanskrit
term for 'agent' is described by grammarians as 'having the law
within it', in other words, containing the rule of action by which
he or she proceeds. In cricket, for example, a batsman 'contains'

the rules of how to bat. The agent, however, in Sanskrit grammar is not the self. He is just the grammatical agent in the sentence. If the batsman intends to strike the ball, then his intention naturally follows from his knowledge of how to bat. He himself does nothing. The ego in its function of a batsman – until he is dismissed! – does it all for him.

Other senses of action
Other senses of 'action' in the English language support the view that the self does nothing. The chemical action of materials on one another is clearly impersonal. Salt acts upon ice to melt it. Of course, salt does not have a self anyway, so this does not take us much further. But the sense of 'action' in a legal case is more useful. The plaintiff's action against the defendant is not the act of an individual. It consists of a lot of procedures, pieces of paper, legal rules and, almost incidentally, people doing things. Most significantly, in the theatre the players act in the action of the play. But they act as Hamlet or Othello, not as themselves. In reality, the actor himself suffers nothing of Hamlet's doubts or Othello's jealousy. However violent or impassioned the action, the actor himself is unmoved. When the final curtain falls, he casts away his costume and make-up and takes a taxi home. At no time did he really believe that he was Hamlet. He was never so identified. When the wise man's life comes to an end, he lays it down like a mask.

The way of action or *karma yoga*
The first six chapters of the *Gita* are said to present the principles of *karma yoga*, or the way of action, whilst the rest deal with the way of devotion (Chs 7–12) and the way of knowledge (Chs 13–18). Each is a way to self-realization and can be followed independently, though all three may be followed together, provided the aspirant sets aside his or her personal desire. Arjuna is directed by Krishna to master the way of action, no doubt in keeping with his role as a *kshatriya*. Three injunctions are given by Krishna; to act

without regard for the fruits of action; to avoid identification with action; and to dedicate action to *Brahman*.

Action regardless of its fruits makes it, in a sense, purposeless. The actor turns his mind away from the consequences of the action, and gives his attention entirely to the action itself. This does not mean that the action has no direction or aim. It simply means that any thought of reward, or of evil consequences also, is banished from the mind.

> 'You have the right to work, to that alone
> To any fruits you have no claim at all,
> So let all hope of benefit be gone'
>
> (*Bhagavad Gita*, II, 47, p. 50)

This indifference is the theme of the poem 'If' by Rudyard Kipling: 'If you can meet with triumph and disaster and treat those two imposters just the same.' It is also inherent in the Kantian concept of duty, whereby action is undertaken purely for duty's sake, without concern for personal gain or loss.

Avoiding identification with an action is to act as though one were a self-realized person, who knows that he does not act at all. It is to act under the principle that 'I do nothing at all', even though one may feel that one does something.

> 'Steadfast in action, he thinks 'I do not act',
> In seeing, hearing, touching, smell or taste,
> In moving, sleeping, breathing in or out,
> In taking and in giving, and in speech,
> Or even in the closing of the eyes,
> He is aware that senses merely move
> Amongst their objects.'
>
> (*Bhagavad Gita*, V, 8–9, p. 64)

Identification is the claim that an action is 'mine'. This claim has no foundation, for the self in reality owns nothing. How could it own anything, since it is everything? All is *Brahman*. Thus the claim of 'mine' limits the person claiming; it makes him believe that he is this body or this mind, this 'doer' or even this particular action. When we identify with a pleasurable act, we find it difficult to abandon because we 'become it'. The smoker cannot give up his cigarettes, the alcoholic his bottle, the lover his mistress. How easily can we give up the roles we play in life, in our families, or professions, or communities?

Yet Krishna was not asking Arjuna to abandon his role as a warrior. On the contrary, he was encouraging him to fulfil it. What he was proscribing was identification with the role. Arjuna should fight and kill, but without believing that he is the killer. The self does not kill. Nor does the self marry, have children, become a doctor or lawyer, or buy a house. Thus to give these things up is not to stop the activities; it is to cease to be identified with them. It is to play the part of a father or a doctor as well as possible, without believing that in reality you are one. Identification is subtle. It is a thing of the mind, a false idea based upon dualism. If I think that my son and I are two, then I try to be a father to him. If I know that he and I are one, I just watch the unfolding of the relationship of father and son.

The third and finest form of the way of action is to dedicate action to *Brahman*.

> '. . . Thus quite unattached,
> He offers Brahman everything he does.'
>
> (*Bhagavad Gita*, V, 9, p. 64)

To the self as *Brahman*, actions are offered or dedicated. It is said that every action is always dedicated to something, usually to our own satisfaction, sometimes to that of others. Krishna demands that Arjuna dedicate only to *Brahman*, his real self. Such actions are cleansed of all impurities. The agent gives up his personal motivation in the action and adopts in its place the motivation – as it were – of *Brahman*. The whole course of what happens in the world is said to be his will. Dedication to *Brahman* is acceptance of this complete flow of events, equivalent to religious dedication to the will of God. Personal desire gives way to the needs of the world.

This abandonment of personal will is demonstrated in a story about the wise man of an Indian village. One day a young unmarried woman, who had recently given birth to a baby boy, accused the wise man of being the father. The mother was poor, so the angry villagers took the baby to the wise man, demanding that he should take responsibility for the child, and bring it up in his house. When they shouted at him that he was the father, all he replied was, 'Is that so?' He took the baby, and it lived with him until it grew up. He gave it the best possible upbringing and education. Then one day the mother, now a mature woman, admitted that the real father had been someone else, and she had wrongly accused the wise man. The villagers marched to his house. 'So you were not the father of that woman's child', they cried, rather shamefacedly. 'Is that so?' said the wise man.

Amongst other things, this story shows how a conviction that the self does not act need not lead to a loss of responsibility. On the contrary, the response is enhanced, since it becomes not 'my response' but a response to whatever is needed by the situation. Instead of the indignation of a wrongly accused individual, the response was a willingness to care for a fatherless child.

The true nature of action

A modern teacher of Vedanta said,

> 'The way to rid oneself from evil is to cultivate the attitude that it is nature that is acting through the body, and not the self.'
>
> (*The Orange Book*, p. 116)

What does this mean? The *Gita* offers an analysis of nature in this context. Actions are chiefly of three kinds, those of the body, those of speech and those of the mind. Each of these three may be called the seat or basis of the action, which constitutes one of the five causes of action. The other four are the 'enjoyer' of action, the various organs, the functions associated with action, and finally the deities that preside over action.

Who is the 'enjoyer'? Not the self, but the ego, together with the limitations it has acquired. When I drive a car, the enjoyer is 'me as a driver'. The various organs are the sense organs, which usually play an important part in action, such as seeing when walking, or hearing when conversing. There are said to be twelve functions available in action. These comprise the five types of deliberate movement – walking, grasping, speaking, excreting and copulating, each utilizing specific organs of the body; in addition, there are five 'breaths' (*prana*), which animate inward and outward breathing, the holding of breath between these, the distribution of food throughout the body, and the 'upward' breath by which life is said to depart on death. The final two functions available in action are discursive mind (*manas*), which controls the senses and formulates, and intelligence (*buddhi*), which reasons, discriminates and creates (*see* pp. 148–50). The fifth cause of action is the presiding deity. In the case of speaking, for example, the god of fire presides. For those who object to the proliferation of gods, this may be understood as a kind of inner force – the fire of speech.

This fairly complex account of the causes of action could be debated at length, especially in relation to scientific and psychological information about the body and mind. However, in the present context what matters is that the five causes of action explain how action comes about. They are, indeed, sufficient conditions for action. There is no need for an acting self. Differences of detail, concerning, for example, the organs and functions, do not affect this cardinal principle of Vedanta. The self is not amongst the causes of action. 'I do nothing at all'. Arjuna is absolved from the guilt of killing.

'. . . and so, whoever thinks,
Without intelligence, of his own self
As agent, fails, through feeble-mindedness,
To see in action how things come to pass;
But he who has no thought of selfishness,
Who, even whilst he kills, remains untouched,
In truth he is not bound, nor does he kill.'

(*Bhagavad Gita*, XVIII, 15–17, p. 123)

Does Vedanta then have an answer to the problem that we did not answer earlier (*see* p. 86) – namely that guilt and shame, reward and blame, punishment and moral responsibility seem meaningless if the self does not act? The answer is that most of these continue to operate, both for the wise man who realizes that he himself does nothing, and for the ignorant who believe that they act. However, the wise man sees that they are all part of the play. He may no longer feel guilt and shame, but he accepts reward and blame, punishment and moral responsibility as a member of a society that needs such concepts. Socrates was a supreme example of such a man. In himself he was totally indifferent towards the charges laid against him at his trial. Yet he allowed the due processes of law to condemn him to death. The self had done nothing. Nor did the self die.

Karma and reincarnation

'Just as a leech supported by a straw goes to the end of it, takes hold of another support and contracts itself, so does the self throw this body aside – make it senseless – take hold of another support, and contract itself. Just as a goldsmith takes apart a little quantity of gold and fashions another – a newer and better – form, so does the self throw this body away, or make it senseless, and make another – a newer and better – form.'

(*Brihadaranyaka*, IV iv 3–4, p. 494)

Thus does the *Brihadaranyaka* describe the endless cycles of life and death, which the embodied soul undergoes, until it finds eventual liberation. The impulsion for this repetition of lives comes from the law of *karma*. So long as the individual self believes that it acts, so long as it is attached to action, it is reborn into the world to experience the effects of its past actions. For every action has two kinds of effects: those that have an impact on other creatures and things, and those that affect the subject of the action, the supposed 'doer'. The former effects are inevitable; the latter kind are not. Only when the agent is attached to the action does it affect him or her later.

We are all aware of the difference between events that 'scar' us deeply and others that do not. If someone to whom we are attached dies, we feel great pain. If a total stranger dies, we are not much affected. Attachment leaves a mark upon the emotional ground (*chitta*) of the individual self (*see* pp. 147–8). Non-attachment leaves nothing there. If the *chitta* is hard, it bears many imprints, like scratches on stone. If it is yielding, like water, impressions do not remain. This is not a matter of whether we respond emotionally, but of what is left behind afterwards.

Ramana Maharshi tells a story which illustrates clearly how our attachment is related to belief, and not necessarily to the facts of the case. Two young men went together on a pilgrimage far from their native village. One was killed in an accident. The other told a man from his village, whom he happened to meet, of his friend's death. This man returned home months before the pilgrim, but made a mistake about the two young men's names. He informed the wrong parents of the death. When the pilgrim returned, he found that his own parents had grieved deeply for the loss of their son, and the dead man's parents had remained content and grateful that their son was safe.

What happens to the marks upon the *chitta*? Vedanta claims that they are retained in the new body that – leechlike – we inhabit when we are reborn in another life. This whole process, whereby actions bear their consequences in future lives, is known as the law of *karma*. Each individual brings with him at birth the effects of his former actions. If he lived well, he brings a good inheritance (*sanskara*); if he lived badly, his inherited lot is dark. *Sanskara* is of the mind and body. It has no bearing on the spirit, which is totally unaffected. Thus the nature of the person, physically and mentally, is determined by his or her previous lives, for effects are carried from life to life, unless they are removed by knowledge.

This doctrine of Vedanta, if difficult for the Western mind to accept, nevertheless has great explanatory power. Where do our capacities and predilections come from, if not from the past? Did God create us sick, as John Milton proposed? Is it chance that makes one person brilliantly gifted and another cast down, devoid of merit? Mozart showed great musical talent when he was three. Perhaps he had studied and practised in previous lives. Einstein discovered special relativity without much advanced training in mathematics and physics. The younger Pitt was Prime Minister at twenty-three. They did not acquire these talents by osmosis. In more general terms, many people feel a certain familiarity with the way their lives turn out. 'I have been here before', wrote Christina Rossetti. 'The things that happen to people are like the people they happen to', said Aldous Huxley.

The moment of death

According to the *Chandogya* Upanishad, it is the conviction that someone has at the moment of death which primarily shapes their next life, for this conviction is derived from how the person has lived. Whatever the mind has dwelt upon during life emerges as this final conviction. If one's thoughts and feelings keep reverting to pleasure, one will be reborn with a body and mind fit only for that, with all its possibly deleterious consequences. If the mind dwelt on love for others, then one may be reborn as a great philanthropist or saint. Only if it dwelt on *Brahman* itself, would one be released from the cycle of rebirth.

Whilst the doctrine of *karma* is a feature of the Upanishads, another Vedantic tradition outlines three paths which the soul may follow after death. First is the path leading to the gods, for those who have led a worthy and god-fearing life. This is associated with the summer solstice, with daytime and light. The second is the path of the fathers, or ancestors, associated with the winter solstice, night-time and darkness. Those who have observed rites properly go this way, and return later to the earth. Thirdly, for those who have led ignorant and dissolute lives, there remains a downward path to the world of animals and plants. All three paths hint at reincarnation of the soul in a new form – divine, human or sub-human.

In the *Mahabharata*, the great king of the Kauravas, Bhisma, prolongs his life by yoga after he is mortally wounded, in order to die in the bright half of the year – to take the path of the gods. But Sankara said that Bhisma did this merely for the sake of his followers, knowing himself that the true 'path' was none of these three. For knowledge of *Brahman* leads not to these, but to freedom from any embodiment. 'The Upanishad denies that there can be any other path to liberation except knowledge.' (*Brahma Sutra Bhasya*, p. 890) On death the realized man goes nowhere, because he remains himself.

Liberation

Liberation then is possible. Teachers of Vedanta compare all actions to the shooting of an arrow. After it is released, the effects are beyond one's control; the arrow does its work. But up to the moment of release, the archer may decline to shoot. The agent may withdraw his mind from the action and its anticipated effects. The sting is drawn from the action by dedicating it to *Brahman*, leaving the agent unmarked. To practise non-attachment to action is to work for liberation. For Vedanta this non-attachment can only arise from real knowledge. Without a knowledge of *Brahman* clearly there can be no dedication to *Brahman*. Equally, with that knowledge, dedication follows naturally. Nevertheless, the aspirant may practise dedication, even when his knowledge is incomplete. Indeed such practice is a vital means of attaining knowledge.

So what happens to the fully realized man who has become liberated from the cycle of rebirth? Does he die immediately, never to be reborn? Of course, he continues living out his present life. What has changed is that he no longer creates any new *sanskara*. His actions have no effect upon him. However, the actions he performed in previous lives continue to have the effect determined by his attachment to them. They are, as it were, built into the body and mind that he brought with him into the present life. Similarly, actions in this life prior to realization may have imparted an imprint on his life. The effects of former actions which are still only held in potential, however, are destroyed on realization. When such a man dies, the whole cycle of effects for him is completed, and none remain to cause a new birth. A striking example of this was given by the life of the great 19th-century teacher of *Advaita*, Ramakrishna, who suffered from cancer of the lip. He regarded this as the consequence of former lives, whilst practising non-attachment in his present life. Sankara states the position explicitly.

> 'After the acquisition of knowledge, those virtues and vices that have not begun to yield their fruits and that were accumulating in earlier lives or even in this life before the dawn of knowledge are alone destroyed, but not so are those destroyed whose results have already been partially enjoyed and by which has been begun this present life in which the knowledge of Brahman arises.'
>
> (*Brahma Sutra Bhasya*, p. 839)

The whole subject of *karma* and liberation may appear complex, but a delightful story about some donkeys makes it all simple. Each day a washerman took his donkeys down to the river, loaded up with washing. One day he was ill, so he asked his son to take the donkeys. His son went out and found that there was no way he could get the donkeys to move. They simply refused to budge. He went back to his father and told him. 'Oh, I forgot to tell you,' the washerman replied. 'Each evening I go out and touch each donkey's feet, as though I am binding them. Then in the morning I do the same, as though releasing them. They won't move until they feel that they have been untied.' The son went back and, when he had touched their feet, the donkeys happily set off for the river. Men and women also think they are bound, when in reality they are completely free.

Time and rationality
How should a Western-educated reader, perhaps well-versed in science, respond to these ideas of *karma* and reincarnation? One reason why they may seem alien is that our concept of time is habitually linear. We think of events occurring in succession in a straight line of time from past to future. Hence a succession of lives seems to conflict irreconcilably with the succession of ordinary events, including the present life. For example, we may ask, 'How can I be reborn, say, later in the 21st century?' or 'Did I live before in the Middle Ages, or in the ancient world?'

But in reality is time linear? Perhaps there are (were/will be) other times, not in a linear relationship to this one. After all, time in dreams is not necessarily in a linear relationship. We may dream of events lasting years 'within' a night's sleep. Similarly, we imagine other times – past and future, and perhaps times purely fictional. To ask when we will be reincarnated in terms of a date in the future may be to misunderstand the whole doctrine.

Moreover, reincarnation is a matter of impressions upon the mind, especially upon the *chitta*. Spirit is not reincarnated, and the body is not the same one as before, since the new one is moulded by the actions of the past. Hence mind, particularly *chitta*, with its concomitants of character and personality, is what provides the continuity from life to life. Yet mind is also what undergoes the states of waking, dreaming and sleeping in which our sense of time varies. So it would not be too surprising if the nature of the time associated with reincarnation were different from our ordinary belief about time.

Finally, *karma* offers a moral dimension lacking in the Western idea of a single lifetime. It is evident that most people do not get their moral deserts in one life. Good men experience untold calamities. Bad men prosper and keep their ill-gotten gains. Perhaps the idea of many lives, in which good and bad actions work themselves out, so that in the long run the good are happy, whilst the bad suffer due punishment, is a more rational one. Nor is such a cyclical eschatology devoid of the concept of mercy. For that would lie in the permanent possibility of evil-doers mending their ways and shaping their own future lives for the better. And, even more, for both good and bad to seek liberation from the whole business of embodied life.

In fact, the Western world has not always believed in one lifetime for each person. The Pythagoreans and Platonists thought of men as living many times on earth. So did the Gnostics and the early Christians, until the time of Clement of Alexandria and Origen in the 3rd century AD. The Christian doctrine of the resurrection of the body can be seen as an attenuated view of reincarnation.

A student of Vedanta, in turn, needs to remember that ultimately *karma* and reincarnation are themselves part of *maya*, or the great illusion of material existence (see pp. 118–20). Only *Brahman* is eternal, unchanging and beyond the dimensions of time and space. Reincarnation occurs only in so far as the material world exists. Both are dependent on *Brahman*, for both are the 'dream' of *Brahman*, which alone is real.

> 'The world is a great show, which God is staging around you in the shape of the universe. But it is a mere show. Your birth is a show, your death is a show. Actually there is neither birth nor death. Know that, and you would be happy.'
>
> (*Birth and Death*, Shantanand Saraswati, p. 11)

The five vestures

> 'He that is here in the human person, and He that is there in the sun, are one. He who knows thus attains, after desisting from this world, this self made of food, attains this self made of vital force, attains this self made of mind, attains this self made of intelligence, attains this self made of bliss.'
>
> (*Taittiriya* Upanishad, II viii 5, *The Eight Upanishads*, Vol I, p. 354)

How can anyone come to see that he himself and 'He that is there in the sun' are one? This verse in the *Taittiriya* comes at the end of a section concerning the five vestures (or sheaths) – namely food, vital force, mind, intelligence and bliss. The purport is that one wins liberation by freeing oneself successively from identification with each vesture, starting with food. When these five limitations cease, there remains no difference between the consciousness of the human being and the consciousness present in the Sun.

Food stands first because the body is made of food. Thus the physical body is the food vesture, having the shape of the human form – head, trunk and limbs. Identification with it takes place in the waking state, when we easily, though not necessarily, think that we are a person of a certain height, weight, physical type and so on. When we recognize ourselves in the mirror, that is the food vesture. So, too, if the body is injured, when we say 'I am hurt'; and when we fear the destruction of the body after death. The body in this sense is lifeless, for the food vesture is the simple physical substance created from food. What animates it, making it a living body, is the second vesture, that of the vital force.

This vesture is said to occupy, as it were, the form of the food vesture, filling its shape from within and constituting more or less its physiology. Whereas the food vesture naturally has the human shape, this second vesture only assumes it, since it is made of air. It comprises the functions that make the body a living organism and enable it to act. The vital or life force, which is the chief breath (*prana*), is central to these. The other four breaths complete it (*see* p. 95). Thus air is said to animate the otherwise lifeless physical body; for example, the five forms of action (*see* p. 95) are dependent upon it. Indeed, movement itself is regarded by Vedanta as an essential quality of air. Identification with this second vesture occurs also in the waking state.

Mind makes up the third vesture. This refers to the discursive mind (*manas*), which has several functions, such as controlling the senses, thinking, imagining, recalling and doubting (*see* pp. 149–50). Identification with mind occurs in both waking and dream states, but is absent in the state of deep sleep. Mind vesture also assumes the human shape, occupying the air vesture from within. In fact, the five vestures closely resemble a set of Russian dolls.

Ramana Maharshi asserts that 'thought builds up the sheaths.' This means that, in a sense, all five vestures, in so far as we are identified with them, seem to be present in the mind vesture. This is not illogical. The sheaths themselves, as individual entities, occur in five different 'materials' – food, air, mind, intelligence and bliss – but identification with them is a thought, and this thought, in relation to any one of the five, occurs in the mind vesture. When identification ceases, the mind vesture continues, but its contents do not then include the particular thought of identification with one or other of the vestures.

Beyond the mind vesture is the vesture of intelligence. This is very much associated with what we ordinarily consider to be self-knowledge. As Ramana Maharshi puts it, this is the 'I-thought', or ego. In this vesture occurs the basic idea of duality that mainly governs our view of ourselves and the world. For the I-thought says 'I and this' – in other words, me and everything else. From this springs our 'knowledge' of the world. From it also arises our recognition of duties in the world. The *Taittiriya* includes in these the performing of sacrifices, which accords with the Vedantic principle that real, or higher, knowledge transcends all duties and rites. Will, too, is said to be a feature of this vesture.

The fifth and final vesture is that of bliss. This is not absolute bliss, which is of the very nature of the self. It is the pleasure and happiness that motivate most people most of the time. At the crudest level it is sensual; at a higher level it is the sense of satisfaction attendant upon a duty properly performed, a skilful piece of work or the knowledge that a loved one is safe. In short, it is the feeling of pleasure or happiness. The Upanishads describe this as a mere fragment of the real and permanent bliss of the self, like a spark from a fire, or a reflection of the Sun. Such fragments are enough to motivate us, and even collectively to inspire such philosophical principles as the Utilitarian one of 'the greatest happiness of the greatest number'. However, even the bliss vesture is a trap for the unwise. Identification with it blocks the way to liberation. Happiness does not have to be destroyed, only the belief that 'I am happy' or 'I enjoy life'. For to believe that the self is happy (or unhappy) stands in the way of the higher knowledge of the truly blissful self. Since the ego is an illusion, so too is its happiness.

As with the analysis of the three states in the *Mandukya* Upanishad, this explanation of the five vestures requires a profound change of viewpoint to be fully appreciated. The vestures are presented as individual limitations on the self. They have the form of an individual man, and the qualities that an individual possesses, such as physiological functions, thoughts, sense of ego and personal happiness. Yet the verse quoted above from the *Taittiriya* refers to one who knows that he is the same as the 'person' in the Sun attaining a self made of food, a self made of vital force and so on. What is attained? Surely Vedanta always insists that the self is already present, not something to be attained. The answer is that the enlightened man attains a universal viewpoint, consequent upon the loss of an individual viewpoint. To 'desist from this world' is to give up the apparent world of the individual, the personal body, personal life and personal mind, instead finding in its place the enormously greater world of a universal body, universal life, reaching even to universal bliss. These, too, are ultimately illusion, but they are the body, life and bliss of the true self, the *Brahman*. Again we may turn to the analogy of the rope and the snake. The illusory snake disappears on the dawning of knowledge. The rope, which is relatively real, remains, though even this is ultimately unreal.

Transcendent and immanent *Brahman*

This understanding of the doctrine of the five vestures is supported by the experience of people such as the writer Thomas Traherne, for whom the universe itself was seen as the body of Man.

> 'You never enjoy the world aright, till the sea itself floweth in your veins, till you are clothed with the heavens, and crowned with the stars: and perceive yourself to be the sole heir of the whole world, and more than so, because men are in it who are every one sole heirs as well as you.'
>
> (Thomas Traherne, *Centuries*, p. 14)

When the individual viewpoint of a separate personal body has been eclipsed by the kind of universal experience that Traherne describes, the whole experience of the personal vestures becomes illusory. Yet what remains – the world seen from a viewpoint which is universal – is not the final reality. It is the level of *maya*, the dream of *Brahman*, and not the pure *Brahman* devoid of all qualities. The snake has gone; the rope remains.

Nevertheless, Vedanta would be incoherent if it presented two levels of illusion without further explanation. Coherence is restored by the distinction made between the *Brahman* as transcendent and the *Brahman* as immanent. The former, known as *Nirguna Brahman*, has no qualities whatsoever, though its threefold nature is existence, knowledge and bliss (*sat–chit–ananda*). The latter, *Saguna Brahman*, is *Brahman*'s dream of the world, known as *maya*. The world is *Brahman*'s dream. Everything in the world consists of mere names and forms. If things like bodies, other material objects and mental experiences are seen correctly, they are just names and forms shaping the dream of *Brahman*. The world is illusion. On this *maya*, or illusion, the individual super-imposes a further layer of falsity. He believes that a mere name or form really exists. He thinks that his body is real, that chairs and tables are real things, that his thoughts have substance. When the truth is established, he sees these things merely as names and forms. He sees the dream of *Brahman* for what it truly is (*see* pp. 118–20).

Maya is perhaps the most difficult of all the concepts of Vedanta. How can *Brahman* be both immanent, as *maya*, and transcendent, as beyond all the created universe? There can be no doubt that *Brahman* is one and not dual. In some sense then it has two aspects, immanent and transcendental. Liberation means both identity with *Nirguna Brahman* and, at the same time, seeing the universe as *Saguna Brahman*. Yet there is no duality.

Obviously any true understanding can only occur in the full experience of self-realization. Nevertheless a simple analogy may make this difficult area of Vedanta a little clearer. Consider the idea of monarchy. It has two aspects. On one hand, there is the monarch as a person. On the other hand, there is the office or function of monarchy. The former is a tangible, living man or woman, observable by others, performing actions, of limited duration and fulfilling, as we say, the office of monarch. The latter is intangible, impersonal, unobservable, inactive, immortal and denoting in itself the very office called monarchy. Yet the monarch is the monarchy. The monarch embodies the office. The monarch and the monarchy are one. When the citizen acknowledges the sovereignty of the monarch, that citizen defers to the monarchy in the form of the monarch. When the liberated man or woman acknowledges unity with the *Nirguna Brahman*, the universe assumes the form of *Saguna Brahman* or *maya*. Liberation is not a void; it is the universe seen aright.

The *Chandogya* Upanishad gives a clue to the concept of *Saguna Brahman* when it describes *Brahman* as 'having the form of consciousness' (III 14 2). This does not, of course, mean that consciousness itself has forms, but that the *Nirguna Brahman*, itself devoid of all qualities, possesses consciousness (*chit*) as one aspect of its nature, and this one indivisible consciousness as *Saguna Brahman* is the single form of *Brahman*. All other forms – creatures, things, qualities and so on – are, as it were, woven on this one seamless form. Space, time, the laws of the universe and everything that they embrace, all occur under the form of consciousness, even though this is not divisible and has no form, just as space is not divisible and has no form. The translation of this key phrase in the *Chandogya* could be rendered as 'having a "light-form" or a "lustre-form"'. For we experience everything, in both waking and dream states, in the light of consciousness, and in the state of deep sleep this light is said to be still there, but without any objects to be experienced. Hence this light by which all things are illuminated and made possible is the one form of the *Brahman*, the substance of *Brahman* as *maya*. He who sees the world as *maya* is liberated, for he is not bound in any way by association with it. He is in the world, but not of it.

Freewill

The question of the freedom of the will presents itself rather differently in Vedanta than in modern Western philosophy, where it is seen usually in terms of determinism – if everything in the universe is governed by causal laws, where is there room for free will? Indian thinkers have seen it more in terms of *karma*. If actions follow naturally and inevitably as the effects of earlier actions, how can anyone will anything else?

Vedanta offers broadly two answers to this problem, one for the case of the ordinary man, one for that of the realized man. Only for the former is free will a problem. The individual asks himself how his actions can be freely chosen, if *sanskara* determines them (*see* pp. 97–8). But who or what makes a choice? It cannot be the real self, for that does nothing, and hence *a fortiori* does not choose. Choosing is a principal function of intelligence (*buddhi*), one of the five causes of action (*see* pp. 94–6). Thus the question of freedom of choice resolves itself into the conditions under which *buddhi* makes choices. When the ego interferes with the operation of *buddhi* by raising unnecessary doubts or introducing irrelevant factors into the situation, then the choice is not made on the basis of what action is appropriate. When the ego allows the choice to be made entirely on this basis, then it is freely made. The situation itself is presented by *sanskara*. One might ask whether the interference or non-interference of ego is also produced by *sanskara*. At this point, however, the real question is 'Who asks that?' What makes a free choice is the absence of interference, not the absence of a cause of the interference. Indeed one might say that the whole problem of free will for the individual can be dissolved by asking who wants to know whether choices are free. If it is only the ego, why worry about the question!

On realization, however, the position is quite different. In one sense the self-realized man loses his free will. He no longer acts from personal motives, even altruistic ones. His personal will is totally subsumed within the will of *Brahman*. But has *Brahman* a will at all? The answer is that the whole course of events in the universe is the will of *Brahman*. Like a leaf that falls into a river, the will of the realized man does nothing of its own beyond following the single flow of universal events. In whatever place, at whatever time, he finds himself, his actions conform to the necessity of the moment. His intelligence has become the universal intelligence, his body and mind instruments of that. It was this that the centurion who said 'I also am a man set under authority' (Luke 7:8) recognized in Christ. 'Nevertheless not as I will, but as thou wilt' (Matthew 26:39) was Christ's prayer in the garden of Gethsemane.

Vedanta claims that every person is at least free to dedicate an action to whatever he or she chooses. This dedication has an effect. It changes the nature of the action, even if outwardly it appears to make no difference. An action dedicated to one's own pleasure, and the very same action dedicated to *Brahman*, have different consequences. Yet though this individual free choice constitutes a kind of freedom of the will, this amounts to no more than a relative freedom. The real question is whether this is used in the search for liberation or for something else. Is the individual exercising his free will in order – paradoxically – to lose his own individuality, or to perpetuate it? Liberation means freedom from all limitations. It is the individual who has the problem of free will. No such problem exists for the self-realized man, for the self is above all questions of choice or lack of choice. His will has become merged with the will of *Brahman*. His choice accords with the natural flow of the universe, unimpeded by personal desires of any kind.

> 'Freewill holds the field in association with individuality. As long as individuality lasts so long there is free will . . . Find out to whom free will or destiny matters . . . To whom do these questions arise? Find out and be at peace.'
>
> (*Talks*, p. 410)

A question may remain concerning the rule of law. Especially in countries subject to English common law, the principle of individual freedom is paramount. Does Vedanta reduce the importance of this, so that tyrannical government could find in it a justification for oppressing the individual? On the contrary, Vedanta asserts the fundamental need for the individual to be free to choose his own course of action. External impediments from those who would inhibit this choice unnecessarily, whether criminals or government officials, are contrary to *dharma*, the true law. Liberation is a matter for individuals to realize for themselves. To think that the State or government can override this is to confuse the issue.

Chapter 6

Nature

Creation

The *Hymn of Creation* in the Rig Veda fuses the poetic inspiration of the earliest Indian thinkers with the spirit of philosophical enquiry that later emerged in the Upanishads.

> 'Then even nothingness was not, nor existence.
> There was no air then, nor the heavens beyond it.
> What covered it? Where was it? In whose keeping?
> Was there then cosmic water, in depths unfathomed?
>
> Then there was neither death nor immortality,
> Nor was there then the torch of night and day.
> The One breathed windlessly and self-sustaining.
> There was that One then, and there was no other.
>
> . . .
>
> But, after all, who knows, and who can say
> Whence it all came, and how creation happened?
> The gods themselves are later than creation,
> So who knows truly whence it has arisen?

Whence all creation has its origin,
He, whether he fashioned it or whether he did not,
He, who surveys it all from highest heaven,
He knows – or maybe even he does not know.'
(from A.L. Basham, *The Wonder that was India*, pp. 247–8)

Though creation myths, such as the emergence of the universe from a golden egg or from a sacrificial horse, are present in Vedantic literature, the Upanishads themselves give short shrift to such imaginative devices, and typically refer instead to the universal self, *Brahman*, and the concept of existence. Even so there are a variety of ways in which creation is related to these fundamentals. The *Aitareya* Upanishad, for example, retains a touch of poetic humour.

In the beginning this was but the Self alone. There was nothing else whatsoever that winked. He thought, "Let Me create the worlds." '

Sankara comments on this verse by explaining that the self remains the same when creation occurs, for the created world is simply the diversification of self 'through the multiplicity of names and forms'. He introduces the analogy of water, which undergoes no change when foam appears upon it. The principle that the self creates without any change of nature is basic to Vedanta, and elsewhere Sankara compares creation to a man dreaming. As he dreams he remains the same, even whilst the contents of his dream spring forth, as if from nowhere, but lit by his own consciousness.

'There are no chariots, nor animals to be yoked to them, nor roads there, but he creates chariots, the animals and the roads. There are no pleasures, joys, or delights there, but he creates the pleasures, joys and delights. There are no pools, tanks, or rivers there, but he creates the pools, tanks and rivers. For he is the agent.'

(*Brihadaranyaka* Upanishad, IV iii 10, pp. 443–4)

This comparison with the dream state helps also to reconcile the idea that *Brahman* does nothing with the idea that it creates, which appears irreconcilable. For dreams are not deliberately made, in the sense in which a craftsman manufactures something. Moreover, one may understand how creation involves no 'doing', for example in the case of the production of an original work of art or writing, when it may take the form of 'appearing', being 'heard' or 'seen' by the author, without his or her doing anything.

Earlier in the *Brihadaranyaka*, however, occurs a rather different account of creation.

'In the beginning, this universe was but the self [Viraj] of a human form. He reflected and found nothing else but himself. He first uttered, "I am he". Therefore he was called *Aham* [I]. Hence, to this day, when a person is addressed, he first says, "It is I", and then says the other name that he may have.'

(*Brihadaranyaka* Upanishad, I iv 1, p. 64)

Here Man plays a crucial role, for he himself, on a universal scale as Viraj, is the source of the created world. He desires a wife, so he divides into two, thus creating a female who fills the whole of space. Between them Viraj and his wife then create other living beings and all the elements.

Later in the *Brihadaranyaka* a more abstract view is stated.

'This self was indeed *Brahman* in the beginning. It knew only Itself as, "I am *Brahman*". Therefore It became all.'

(*Brihadaranyaka* Upanishad, I iv 10, p. 100)

Becoming without change of nature is once again the key notion in the Vedantic conception of creation. *Brahman* does not make or fashion the universe. It is rather an expression or manifestation of himself. *Nirguna Brahman* becomes *Saguna Brahman*. There is also a parallel here between the primeval creation and the self-realization of a man. The man who knows that 'I am *Brahman*' becomes all this universe.

The order of creation

Yet in other verses the Upanishads talk of creation as a kind of process or progression through stages. The elements emerge in a definite order from *Brahman*, and Man as a living creature comes rather late in the day!

> 'From that *Brahman*, which is the Self, was produced space. From space emerged air. From air was born fire. From fire was created water. From water sprang up earth. From earth were born herbs. From herbs was produced food. From food was born man. That man, such as he is, is a product of the essence of food.'
>
> (*Taittiriya* Upanishad, II i1, in *The Eight Upanishads*, Vol 1,
> p. 287)

In this account the universe emerges from *Brahman* in sequence, not 'like a handful of jujubes thrown down' (*Mundaka*, I i7, commentary). The whole question of order or succession highlights a central aspect of the Vedantic principle of creation. Order can be temporal or abstract. Temporal order implies that the creator existed first in time, and subsequently created the universe and its contents in temporal sequence. Such a view is a naïve interpretation of the Upanishads. Their import is rather that creation has an abstract order in the sense of ontological priority or dependence. Space cannot exist without *Brahman*, for in the absence of consciousness there is nothing at all, not even space. Air cannot exist without space, since it occupies space. Similarly, fire requires air, for heat is only generated by movement; water requires fire, for it reflects light; and earth requires water, for it disintegrates without it. That herbs need earth and Man needs food are yet more obvious.

Abstract order or succession implies that *Brahman* itself did not exist before the universe in time. How can this be? *Brahman* was not temporally first. It is eternal, or beyond time altogether. Time is no more than a condition in which the universe exists. Hence the creation did not emerge at a point in time; nor will it end at a point in time. It is everlasting. Indeed, it has been described as a beginningless, endless superimposition on *Brahman*. And yet the *Upanishads* often describe it as having its origin and dissolution in *Brahman*, and being sustained by *Brahman* in between. Here, too, the meaning is not temporal, except in so far as cycles within time are concerned (*see* pp. 131–6). Creation emerges, is sustained and dissolves in a non-temporal order. Vedanta uses analogies to demonstrate this.

> 'The metaphors of the spinning of the web by a spider, the bearing of the child by the mother, the production of notes from musical instruments, attempt to bring out the intimate relationship between the cause and the effect. It is the *tadatmya* or oneness between *Brahman* and the world that is conveyed in all this wealth of symbol and image. The external world is not something separate, existing side by side with the *Atman*. The ultimate ground of being, *Brahman*, and the empirical state of being, the world, are not different. The world of plurality can be reduced without residuum into the everlasting one, *Brahman*.'
>
> (S. Radhakrishnan, *Indian Philosophy*, Vol I, p. 183)

Material and efficient causation

Such an explanation applies also to the additional concept of a creator god, Brahma, earlier known as Prajapati. He is not seen as the source of all creation, but as the creator of the universe from a primeval material or chaos. When he creates he does not bring forth something out of nothing; like an artist, he fashions or moulds the material. Similarly the great god Vishnu sustains the creation, and Siva destroys it. These three represent powers by which *Brahman* itself brings about the threefold 'act' of creation, sustenance and dissolution.

In this light, Vedanta sees no need for there also to be an initial substance other than *Brahman* from which all is created. *Brahman* does not shape the universe. Reality is one. There can be no primeval substance or material co-extensive with *Brahman*, for it is the one eternal substance itself. *Brahman*'s manifestation is the appearance of this substance as names and forms, as *Saguna Brahman*, which is the universe. Hence *Brahman* is the material cause of the universe, in the Aristotelian sense. The world is constructed out of the consciousness of *Brahman*, just as a clay pot is constructed out of clay. Take away the clay and there is no pot. Take consciousness away and there is no world. A pot is a mere form of clay. It may be transformed into a plate or a brick by the imposition on the clay of a new form. Thus the forms in the world come and go, while consciousness remains.

Although the question of whether everything originates in a complete void or nothingness is raised in the Upanishads, they always insist that *Brahman* is the ultimate reality.

> 'My son! In the beginning, there was mere being, one without a second. Some say there was mere nothing, nothing whatsoever; that everything has come out of nothing.'

> 'But how can that be true, my son', said Uddalaka; 'how could that which is, come from that which is not? I put it otherwise; in the beginning there was mere being, one without a second.'

> (*The Ten Principal Upanishads*, p. 86)

How can something come out of nothing? Sometimes the words '*sat*' (existence) and '*asat*' (non-existence) are taken to refer to existence in the world. In which case *Brahman* itself is said to be neither '*sat*' nor '*asat*'. However, the possibility of ultimate non-existence, or nothingness, is ruled out on the grounds that since appearances exist – albeit we may not know what they are – they must inhere in or be dependent upon a substance, which is *Brahman* or pure being. The idea of the phenomenol logically depends upon that of the noumenol.

Is *Brahman* the efficient cause of the universe also? Vedanta insists that it is. Yet here the relationship between cause and effect is more subtle than in the material case. *Brahman* is not like the potter who moulds the clay; nor like the acorn that becomes an oak tree. For *Brahman* does nothing and suffers no loss when it creates. It 'makes' the world as sunlight makes a mirage in the desert; or as the ocean makes waves; or as a spider makes a web from its own substance.

Vedanta does not then give a single precise account of how creation occurs. Rather it states certain fundamental principles: that *Brahman* is the source of everything; that the universe is a manifestation or expression of *Brahman*; that nothing can emerge from a void; and that there is a definite ontological order in creation.

'Who wants to know?'

Phenomena are endless, says Ramana Maharshi. Therefore why look outwards and go on trying to explain them *ad infinitum*? His answer to the whole question of creation is to find the real 'I' or self, since the creation is contained within it. Kant might have agreed. If time is in us, as Kant argued, then how can we find the origin of all things at an objective temporal beginning?

Maharshi's technique of asking 'Who wants to know?' is applicable in this case. Who asks when and how creation took place? It is the ego, not the real self. Therefore one should look for the questioner and then search for his origin. How did he – the ego

– begin? What sustains him? How is he to be dissolved? These questions lead to reality; the others lead nowhere. Physicists may propound brilliantly complex theories about the origin of the observable universe. Yet they do not tell us about the observer of it. Nor do they tell us whence it comes now, in the present moment, except perhaps to say from the past.

Such an approach, inherent in *Advaita* Vedanta, explains why the Upanishads do not spend many words on the nature of the creation. They allow for a few myths, but they revert always to the self or *Brahman*. As Maharshi says,

> 'The riddle of the creation of the world is thus solved if you solve the creation of the 'I'. So I say, find your Self.'
>
> (*Talks*, p. 449)

Nature as *maya*

Once a man cleverly defrauded a local craftsman. The man's children said that they would like some toy coins to play with. He went to the local potter and asked him to make five hundred imitation rupees in clay for a small charge of a few rupees. When he returned for them, they were not quite finished. 'When will you give me my five hundred rupees?' he asked in a loud voice. 'I promise to give them to you tomorrow', said the potter. There were other people in the shop who heard all this. Later the man successfully sued the potter for five hundred rupees, calling on witnesses from the shop to prove his case.

What is the point in this story? It demonstrates how problems and difficulties arise from mistaking what is illusory for what is real. If you believe that this world is the final reality, most people will support your view, and you have to accept the consequences of your error. The world is, of course, an extremely effective illusion. It takes a great deal of understanding and practice to realize that it is only *maya*, the dream of *Brahman*. The root of the word *maya* is *ma*, meaning 'to measure', for the world is said to be measured out in its innumerable forms by *Brahman*.

Maya is most easily appreciated as nature, in the sense of all the powers or forces of natural phenomena. Sanskrit uses the word *prakriti* for these, so that *maya* may be said to be *prakriti* seen as the dream of *Brahman*. However, the Vedantic concept of nature is different from our rather vague notion, and in particular it does not draw the familiar Western distinction between Man and nature. Man as a physical, mental and emotional creature is entirely included within it. In the abstract order of creation, nature is the first emanation from *Brahman*. Yet this initial movement does not involve the manifestation of *Brahman* in a space-time world. At this primary stage, nature remains unmanifest, as a kind of potential, from which manifest creatures can be drawn. This idea is similar to the Platonic concept of 'the original of the universe [which] contains in itself all intelligible beings' (*Timaeus*, 30). Although all created things lie in potential within it, yet it is completely undifferentiated, like the stone which contains all the manifold forms of the sculptor's art.

From this unmanifest potential the creative process moves to the manifestation of nature. This is the stage when things begin to be measured out through three basic forces of nature, known by the virtually untranslatable Sanskrit word *guna* (*see* pp. 123–6). Mind as emotion, intelligence and discursive power precedes the five elements of space, air, fire, water and earth, which constitute the material world. Man's nature is a microcosm of the universal nature, but in one crucial respect it differs. Unmanifest nature contains a seed of ignorance, which is said to have no cause. In Man it gives rise to the ego, the false idea of self, which motivates all action, until knowledge of reality destroys the belief in it. In nature itself, on a macroscopic scale, the equivalent of this false unity in Man is the unity of natural phenomena implicit in the idea of a 'mind of nature'. On this universal scale, however, there is no falsity.

Everything except *Brahman* itself is nature. For it is through nature that *Brahman* creates the universe. Hence all things – men, animals, plants and inert things – are all nature. Dualistic (*dvaita*) versions of Vedanta draw upon this comprehensive idea to derive an ontological distinction between *Brahman* and nature. *Advaita* Vedanta rejects this temptation. It claims that nature never ceases to be *Brahman* in the guise of *maya*. Nature in its entirety is an illusion, like the rope seen as a snake. It does exist, but its existence is dependent upon the *Brahman*. The snake exists as an illusory snake, entirely dependent upon the rope. The mirage in the desert exists as a mirage, dependent upon rays of light, but not as an actual oasis.

A great deal follows from this conception of nature as *maya*. Everything that happens is done by nature. *Brahman* does nothing. When someone walks, eats, thinks or decides, for example, it is just as much an action of nature as when a plant grows or an apple falls to the ground. All laws, whether physical or mental, are laws of nature. All causes and effects operate in nature. If Man tries to interfere, his interference is governed by natural law. There is, however, no purpose that stems from nature itself. To ask why nature acts as it does in a teleological sense is to forget its dependence upon *Brahman* (except in so far as functional explanations of parts of an organism are concerned). Nature exists and acts for *Brahman*. Its actions are the will of *Brahman*. What can be the end of such a will? *Brahman* is an end in itself: *sat–chit–ananda* (existence–knowledge–bliss).

Appearance of and appearance to

Nature is the appearance of *Brahman*. But to whom does *Brahman* appear? The simple answer is to us, we human beings. Thus to call nature an appearance seems to have two aspects – an appearance of and an appearance to. This implies a duality between *Brahman* and ourselves. *Brahman* exists as an appearance and we exist as observers of this appearance. The very concept of appearance seems to contain a duality. We experience this apparent duality whenever we feel ourselves to be conscious beings looking out at the works of nature. We may even believe that the creature we observe is an appearance of *Brahman*, but we still feel that the conscious 'I' that observes is different from the consciousness, or whatever lies 'behind' the appearance. We regard it as an appearance *of* one thing appearing *to* another thing.

The Vedantic remedy for this dualistic thinking is to remember that consciousness is one. What sees the appearance is the same as what lies behind it. Since consciousness is everywhere, this is not difficult to understand as an idea. A piece of reasoning may take this further. I am a witness of the appearance. But this need not mean that the witnessing takes place within space, that there are subject and object, both in space. If the self contains space, as Vedanta (and Kant) assert, then the appearance, which is spatial, is actually in the self. What lies 'beyond' the appearance is this same self which contains it as witness. The great illusion is that space and time are themselves real, when they too are aspects of *maya*. Nature includes space and time, for they are contained in potential *prakriti* and emerge as the bounds of its manifest form. Once this is understood, the non-dualistic notion of nature as the dream of *Brahman* becomes intelligible.

Nature and liberation

Another traditional story emphasizes the importance of becoming indifferent to nature. A man was crossing a dry area on horseback, and he and his horse became thirsty. They were directed to a place which had a water pump. The man satisfied his thirst from the pump, but the horse refused to drink, because whenever the pump worked there was a loud noise, which frightened it. Either the horse drank despite the noise, or it had nothing to drink. It could not overcome its fear, so it went without.

We are like the horse if we cannot free ourselves from identification with, or attachment to, natural things, such as the pleasures and pains of the body or mind. We will never experience the absence of body or mind. Liberation is available only in life, not in death. Since nature is beginningless and endless – its creation is not a temporal process – liberation from nature cannot arise from its cessation. Freedom from nature is only found by learning to be indifferent, both to its blandishments and to its strictures.

Nor can we select which aspects of nature to disregard. The laws of nature do not allow that we indulge pleasure and become indifferent to pain. Either we are attached to both or we become indifferent to both. Nor can we treat disaster as an imposter and continue to pursue success as genuine. Nature herself is indifferent to our pleas for preference, as we all know from hard experience. Yet she keeps at a distance if we really show an absence of all attachment.

The path to liberation is therefore through reason, which discriminates between the reality of *Brahman* and the unreality of the ego and its personal 'world', and through the practice of detachment, which releases the grip of *maya*. Since nature, or *maya*, is closest of all to *Brahman*, the realization that it is unreal is the final step to liberation. This cannot be made by the individual, for it amounts to giving up individuality itself, or renouncing all belief in an individual nature. In the earlier stages of liberation the individual makes a kind of effort. This is not so much a positive act of trying, or will power, as a releasing or letting go. Saying 'Not this, not this' to a particular attachment, such as the pleasure of taste, requires only that identification with it is dropped. What is given up is a sense of possession of personal experiences. However, for the final step that goes beyond nature itself to complete freedom in unity with *Brahman*, no effort of any kind by the individual is possible. The individual can only draw near, as it were, to *Brahman*, and await what might be called the grace of God.

A story illustrates the best approach to this apparent helplessness of the individual in the face of intractable nature. There was a holy man, who practised meditation every day seated under a tamarind tree. One day an angel, called Narada, appeared to him, and asked if he wanted to send a message to *Brahman*. The holy man said that he would like to ask when he might finally meet *Brahman*. Narada took the message and returned later, warning the holy man that he would not welcome the reply. '*Brahman* says that he will meet you after as many years as there are leaves on this tamarind tree.' The tree had many thousands of small leaves. To Narada's surprise the holy man began to dance in an ecstasy of delight. 'Did you hear the message correctly? You will have to wait for thousands of years', Narada asked. 'Yes', replied the holy man. 'All that matters is that *Brahman* will meet me. He will never let me down.' Whereupon *Brahman* appeared in person. Narada was rather put out by this. 'You have made me seem like a liar!', he exclaimed angrily. 'In a special case like this the ordinary rules of space and time do not apply. This man is truly devoted to me, so he and I may meet straight away' was *Brahman*'s response.

Gunas

Everything except the transcendent *Brahman* is nature (*prakriti*). The three *gunas* constitute this nature, even in its unmanifest form as the potentiality of all created things. For although unmanifest nature is completely undifferentiated, yet the *gunas* as fundamental forces, or energies, exist as its constituents in a state of equilibrium. When the equilibrium is disturbed, they become manifest as threefold, and while they remain so disequilibrium continues. Hence when the potential of nature is realized in created things, like men, animals, plants or minerals, it is always in a condition of change or movement. Nothing in nature stays precisely the same.

Although the doctrine of the three *gunas* may be implicit in the Upanishads, it was developed principally by Samkhya philosophers and subsequently by Sankara. The *Bhagavad Gita* also has much to say about the action of *gunas*. They are denoted by the Sanskrit words *sattva*, *rajas*, and *tamas*, and these too, like *guna*, have no equivalents in Western languages. This linguistic fact seems to count against the claim of Vedanta that the *gunas* are the basic ingredients of the created world. How could this be unknown to Western civilization? If it had been known in the West at some time, surely there would be traces of the doctrine in our language.

The number three does, however, appear in many fundamental areas of Western life and thought. It is found, for example, in the three persons and the three genders of grammar, the three forces of positive, negative and neutral, the trinity of Christianity, the thesis, antithesis and synthesis of dialectical philosophy, the three Graces, the three dimensions of space, the triangle as the basis of much geometry and trigonometry and no doubt in many other areas of mathematics.

Sattva, rajas and *tamas* are neither substances, qualities nor properties, in the usual sense of those terms. Since *gunas* cannot exist on their own, but only as a triad, they cannot be called substances. Another meaning of the word *guna* is 'thread' or 'strand', as in a cord or rope, which implies their interdependence in the 'rope' of *prakriti*. Nor are the *gunas* qualities, for of what would they be qualities? As the very constituents of nature, they are not mere qualities of it, still less can they be qualities of *Brahman*, for it has none. Qualities are limitations. Whatever is red, for example, cannot be another colour. And *Brahman* is absolutely unlimited.

The three *gunas* can be described, however, particularly through their effect on the entities of nature which embody them: *sattva* is variously described as goodness, lightness, happiness, peacefulness or stillness; *rajas* is forcefulness, movement, action, passion, energy, activity or agitation; *tamas* is inertia, darkness, sloth, dissolution or carelessness. Such terms invite value judgments. *Sattva* is often regarded in Vedantic literature as especially worthy or valuable, and *tamas* as harmful and to be avoided. Strictly, though, all three *gunas* are simply constituents of nature with determinate effects, not all of which are predictably good or bad. Indeed, sometimes all three are understood to have both divine and demonic attributes. Thus divine *sattva* may promote well-being and even liberation, whilst demonic *sattva* creates a kind of Dr Pangloss illusion of everything being for the best in the best of all possible worlds. Divine *rajas* is like the anger of Christ in the temple, which swept away corruption and greed; whereas demonic *rajas* drives destructive forces, such as the ambition which ignores the rights of others. Divine *tamas* may be, for example, the sleep that restores strength and energy; while demonic *tamas* may take the form of outright hatred and of neglect of civilized values.

The physical world exhibits all three *gunas* at any one time. Since they always exist in a state of disequilibrium, one is always predominant. This largely determines the character of the physical thing or event concerned. (Further analysis, according to the relative strengths of the other two *gunas*, is possible.) *Sattva* is predominant in events such as the rising and setting of the Sun, in the season of Spring, in the beauty of flowers or the singing of birds. *Rajas* predominates in storms, earthquakes, the season of Summer, the speed of a horse or the waves of the sea. When *tamas* exceeds the other two then there may be night-time, Winter, sleep, death or the hardness of stone.

Clearly, humans are also subject to the same influence of *gunas*. Body, mind and heart respond to the dominance of one *guna*. We may feel physically light or healthy under *sattva*, energetic or restless under *rajas*, and heavy or lazy under *tamas*. Mentally *sattva* makes us bright and attentive, *rajas* excited and overactive, *tamas* dim and unperceptive. We experience emotions like love and delight, attachment and anger, hatred and envy under the respective *gunas*. Many other states could be categorized. Extreme conditions of divine ecstasy, hyperactivity and clinical depression suggest extremities of *guna* imbalance.

The *Bhagavad Gita* describes at length how the *guna* balance enters into such things as faith, worship, sacrifice, speech, food and the offering of gifts.

> 'That gift most properly due in time and place,
> Offered to one most worthy to receive,
> Without regard to any recompense,
> Is held to be a truly *sattvic* gift;
> But if one gives expecting some return,

> Or benefit, or gives reluctantly,
> That gift is called *rajasic*. One given
> At an inauspicious time, or unfit place,
> To undeserving men, or carelessly,
> Or even with contempt, is *tamasic*.'
> 　　　　　(*Bhagavad Gita*, 17, 20–2, p. 119)

Reference is also made in the *Gita* to the effect of the *guna* balance at the time of death. Although, as discussed earlier (*see* pp. 98–9), the dominant idea held in the mind of a dying man or woman governs the next birth, the *gunas* play a part in this, for the idea is itself coloured by them. As universal constituents, they have entered the mind throughout life and remain there at the time of death.

> 'If death confronts the soul when *sattva* rules,
> It reaches then that heaven, devoid of sin,
> Where dwell the worshippers of highest gods;
> If at a time of *rajas*, it is born
> Among those bound to action; whilst that one
> Who dies in *tamas* finds a brutish womb.'
> 　　　　　(*Bhagavad Gita*, 14, v. 14–15, p. 108)

This is not a deterministic theory of how the succession of lives occurs. Sankara emphasizes that it is attachment to the *gunas* that gives them their potency in determining the future destiny of the dying man. If ideas of virtue or purity are dwelt upon in life, the soul goes to a future life of righteousness. If it was identified with achieving selfish ends, or with mere bodily pleasure, then it goes to a life of continuous activity, or of ignorance and pain.

Freedom from the *gunas*

For Vedanta the whole doctrine of the *gunas* serves one purpose. It is elaborated in the *Gita* and elsewhere in order to show that the self is beyond the *gunas*. Self alone is untainted by them. By

consciousness they may be observed and transcended. It is a mark
of a realized man to be completely indifferent to the presence or
absence of any particular *guna* balance. He does not rejoice when
sattva rules, nor lament the excesses of *rajas* or the darkness of
tamas. Even as he observes them in his own body, mind and
emotions, he remains indifferent. By the Lord Krishna such a man
is especially loved.

> 'He who does not agitate the world,
> Nor whom the world disturbs, unmoved by fear,
> Beyond impatience, pleasure or regret:
> Such a one is specially dear to Me.
> He who depends on nothing, pure at heart,
> Who does not hesitate when called to act,
> Without anxiety or desire to please,
> Whose undertakings offer no reward:
> Such a one is specially dear to Me.'
>
> (*Bhagavad Gita*, 12, 15–16, pp. 101–2)

For those who are so steadfast, a life unmoved by the play of the
gunas has become natural. They do not strive to achieve this divine
indifference. It is natural to them, for they have realized the one
true nature of existence, knowledge and bliss. From these
Olympian heights the concerns of the world recede into insignificance or – more accurately – into unreality. Descriptions of this
sublime lack of attachment, in literature such as the *Gita*, the
Ramayana and the *Mahabharata*, serve as an ideal to guide the
aspirant. Liberation becomes a practical condition, attainable in life
by following the example of one who has demonstrated it.

In the *Ramayana*, Prince Rama, son of King Dasaratha, is about
to be installed as heir to the throne in the royal city of Ayodhya,
when one of Dasaratha's two wives, Kaikeyi, demands that her son,
Baratha, is installed in Rama's place. Earlier she had saved
Dasaratha's life, and won from him the promise to grant her any
two requests that she might choose. Jealous for her son, Baratha,

she demands his installation as heir, and that Rama be banished instantly to the dense forest of Dandaka for fourteen years. Dasaratha is utterly downcast by Kaikeyi's demands, for he is bound by the law of *dharma* (righteousness) to keep his word, yet loves his son Rama deeply and despairs at the prospect of exiling him.

Rama himself restores the situation. He entirely concurs with his father's wish to keep his word. He bears no resentment towards Kaikeyi, nor towards his half-brother, Bharata. On the contrary, he reminds all concerned that he and they are no more than embodiments of the one self that has no concern with worldly affairs. Each faces his or her own *karma*. For Rama himself it was installation as heir to the throne, and now it is exile to the forest. His wife, Sita, and his brother, Lakshmana, insist on accompanying him. Undisturbed, indeed joyous, Rama leaves the city of Ayodhya for fourteen years in the wilderness of the forest of Dandaka. For him the *sattva* of royalty, honour and fame, the *rajas* of power, ambition and anger, the *tamas* of envy, despair and discomfort are of no consequence. In his love for *Brahman* that lives in the hearts of his friends and foes alike, Rama is inured to these passing shadows of worldly existence. He reminds his own mother, Kausalya, who begs him to remain, of the transience of life.

> 'Living beings who are subject to their *karma* cannot always live in the same situation, as different environments are required for the experience of the fruits of their *karmas*. So it is not given to them to live always with the same people in the same place . . . Men subject to *karma* are like boats caught in a current of water. They go in different directions according to the speed and direction of the water. And, after all, fourteen years will pass away like a moment. O mother! Abandon grief and permit me to go. If you do so, I shall be able to live in the forest in peace.'
>
> (*Adhyatma Ramayana*, p. 70)

In the West, the ability to bear suffering has always attracted great interest, exemplified above all by the death of Christ on the Cross, but also by the saints and martyrs of the Church and by people who have triumphed over terrible wounds or diseases. Vedanta would portray these as cases of people who have risen above the *gunas* by becoming – briefly or permanently – identified with the self which transcends nature. Thus the self does not suffer; only the body, mind and heart experience pain or anguish. In Catholic theology, Christ has two natures: that of Man suffers; that of God is above all suffering. Hence the Incarnation redeems mankind by accepting as a man the pain incurred by the sins of others, whilst himself remaining in his divine nature above sin.

The expressions *saguna* and *nirguna* are explained by this notion of transcendence. The former means 'with the *gunas*'; the latter 'beyond the *gunas*'. *Brahman* in its essence is *nirguna*. When understood as the manifested world of names and forms, it is associated, as *maya*, with nature (*prakriti*) and, therefore, with the *gunas*. To be free is to know that the world is *Saguna Brahman* and thus to realize one's identity with *Nirguna Brahman*.

The analogy of a house illustrates the three *gunas*. Man lives in a house with three storeys. He may choose to spend his time in any one of them. In the middle room he does his daily work, for this is the home of *rajas*, or activity. Below is his bedroom, where he sleeps in *tamas*. If he is lazy and lets desire rule his life, he stays down there most of the time, and the house is not cleaned and eventually falls into ruin. On the top floor there is the peace and light of *sattva*. He may go there at any time. If he does so, his work and sleep below will be finer and clearer. A rational man spends a regular part of his day on the top floor, studying or meditating, much of his time working attentively on the middle floor, and gets a measured night's sleep below.

The three *gunas* can also be likened to the three great gods Vishnu, Brahma and Siva. The power of *rajas* is the creative force of Brahma, that of *sattva* fulfils the sustaining and protective function of Vishnu, whilst that of *tamas* enables Siva to bring the world to an end in total withdrawal into *Brahman*. This cosmological conception is reflected in lesser events. For anything to arise, be maintained and fall, such forces are required. Civilizations, cultures and nations undergo cycles of creation, sustenance and dissolution. So do individual human lives and those of animals and plants, as Shakespeare knew well:

> 'When I perceive that men as plants increase,
> Cheered and checked even by the self-same sky;
> Vaunt in their youthful sap, at height decrease,
> And wear their brave state out of memory'
>
> (Sonnet 15)

All can be seen as subject to this great triad of forces. Religions, such as those of the ancient Greeks and Romans, exhibit ideas of gods presiding over these movements. Perhaps today we take the threefold cycle of conception, growth and death so much for granted that we look for no explanation beyond those of biology and other physical sciences. This leaves us with little choice but to submit to the inexorable demands of passing time.

Chapter 7

Time

Historical ages (*Yugas*)

Vedanta rejects the modern Western concept of linear time, a straight line along which:

> '. . . the world moves
> In appetency, on its metalled ways
> Of time past and time future'
> (T.S. Eliot, *Four Quartets*, 'Burnt Norton', p. 18)

Instead it views time as a manifestation of *Brahman*, created and destroyed over and over again, together with all that has temporal form – the world and its contents. Moreover, time is not the merely passive receptacle of creatures and events, but actually forms them.

> 'It is Time which produces all creatures and again devours them. Time is the origin of all creatures; Time is that which makes them grow; Time is that which is their destroyer; and lastly it is time that is their ruler. Subject to pairs of opposites (such as heat and cold, pleasure and pain, etc.), creatures of infinite variety rest on Time according to their

own natures (without being otherwise than how they have
been ordained by supreme *Brahman*.)'

(*Mahabharata*, IX, p. 178)

Time, once created, proceeds by a series of cycles, which are themselves contained one within another. They are given with mathematical precision in the *Mahabharata* and elsewhere. A *mahayuga*
of 4,320,000 years contains four successive ages, which descend
in length of time in the ratio of 4:3:2:1. Their respective lengths
are 1,728,000 years for the golden (*krita*) age; 1,296,000 for the
silver (*treta*) age; 864,000 for the bronze (*dvapara*) age; and
432,000 for the iron (*kali*) age. At the end of an iron age, the cycle
repeats with a new golden age. One thousand *mahayugas* (or one
kalpa) form one day of the creator god, *Brahma*. Three hundred
and sixty days and nights of *Brahma* (720,000 *mahayugas*) make
a year of *Brahma*. 100 years of *Brahma* are the life of *Brahma*,
which amounts to 311,040,000 million years, a time span greatly
in excess of current Western theories about the life of the cosmos.
(A subsidiary analysis of a day of *Brahma* divides it into fourteen
manvantaras, each consisting of seventy-one *mahayugas*.)

Humanity is the dominant, indeed the defining, factor in the
four ages from golden to iron. Each is described in terms of the
conditions of human society, classes and individuals. The symbol
of a bull, representing virtue, encapsulates the changes from one
age to another. In the *Srimad Bhagavatam* its four feet are said
to be austerity, purity, charity and truthfulness. An evil man, named
after the final age, Kali, cuts off three feet in turn, until a good
king, Pariksit, forcibly intervenes and prevents him from destroying
the last remaining foot of truthfulness. Kali begs for mercy. The
king offers him those realms where gambling, drinking, inhuman
treatment of women and cruelty to animals are rife. Kali demands
more – the regions of falsehood, pride, lust, jealousy and enmity.
'Hence, if a man would not be overpowered by Kali (in the iron
age), he must shun these evils.' The king then restores the four
legs of the bull, so that a new *mahayuga* may begin.

The *Laws of Manu* also use the image of the bull, but here it stands for *dharma*, the universal law of righteousness (*see* pp. 195–8). In the *Laws*, the only surviving virtue in the iron age is liberality, rather than truthfulness.

> 'In the *krita* age *dharma* is four-footed and entire, and so is truth; nor does any gain accrue to men by unrighteousness. In the other three ages, by reason of unjust gains, *dharma* is deprived successively of one foot, and through the prevalence of theft, falsehood, and fraud the merit gained by men is diminished by one fourth in each. Men are free from disease, accomplish all their aims, and live four hundred years in the *krita* age, but in the *treta* and in each of the succeeding ages their life is lessened by one quarter . . . One set of duties is prescribed for men in the *krita* age, different ones in the *treta* and in the *dvapara*, and again another set in the *kali*, in proportion as those ages decrease in length. In the *krita* age the chief virtue is declared to be the performance of austerities, in the *treta* divine knowledge, in the *dvapara* the performance of sacrifices, in the *kali* liberality alone.'
>
> (*Laws*, I, 81–3, 85–6, pp. 22–4)

The great epic of the *Mahabharata* is set in the bronze (*dvapara*) age, and tells the story of the mighty warriors who clashed on the field of Kurikshetra. Not only does it provide a rationale for the final descent into the iron age, as standards of conduct in both peace and war decline; it also offers descriptions of all four ages and occasional explanations of the causes of each. In the golden age, the one eternal spiritual teaching was present without the division of the Veda into four. All men and women followed it and, therefore, 'there was no need of religious acts'. There were no gods, nor demons. The only merit was in renouncing the world. Manual labour, and buying and selling did not take place, for all necessities of life were freely available. The human senses did not degenerate, nor did disease weaken the body. No malice, pride, hypocrisy, discord, ill-will, cunning, fear, misery, envy, nor covetousness existed anywhere. Four classes of people – the wise (*brahmanas*), the ruling warriors (*kshatriyas*), the merchants and farmers (*vaisyas*) and those whose function was to serve (*sudras*) – fulfilled the duties which accorded with their nature. The manners and customs of all were suited to the attainment of *Brahman*, and to this end all were devoted. The voice, pronunciation and minds of all men became clear and cheerful. Their meditation was upon the mantra of *OM*. Recognition of the identity of the self with *Brahman* was the distinctive mark of the golden age.

In the *Srimad Bhagavatam* a rather different vision of the golden age is presented:

> 'In the beginning, in the golden age, men had but one caste, known as Hamsa (meaning 'swan', a symbol of the self). All were equally endowed with knowledge, all were born knowers of truth; and since this was so the age was called *krita*, which is to say 'attained'. In that primeval age, Om was the Veda; and I was duty, in the aspects of austerity, purity, charity and truthfulness. Men were pure, and were given to divine contemplation. It was their pleasure to meditate constantly on me (i.e. Krishna) – the pure, the absolute.'
>
> (*Srimad Bhagavatam*, p. 251)

Thus, according to this source, division into the four classes first appeared in the silver age, with the need for specialized duties, such as the pursuit of meditation and truthfulness by the *brahmanas*, fortitude and leadership by *kshatriyas*, wealth and charity by *vaisyas* and service and humility by *sudras*.

In the *Mahabharata* the silver age is marked by the emergence of doubt, which remains until the end of the iron age. Sacrifices are introduced. Virtue decreases by one quarter. Men still look for the truth, but now they follow religious rites. They seek ends other than *Brahman*, using gifts as a means to achieve them. The four classes adhere to their respective duties; however, the king amongst the warriors acquires a new importance. He takes care of seven things: his own self, his counsellors, his treasury, the award of punishments, his friends, the provinces and his capital city. The earth now requires tillage.

By the time of the bronze age, virtue has lost a further quarter. The Veda becomes divided into four parts. Some men retain the knowledge of all four; some forget them all. Life becomes more complicated, as new ends are desired and new means devised. Though asceticism and the offering of gifts remain, such behaviour is influenced by passion. Diseases multiply. Lust is established. Natural calamities grow apace. Afflicted with all this, people take to penance. Though they continue to offer sacrifices, they do so often in order to enjoy life or to attain heaven. Men degenerate as a consequence of impiety.

We live in the age of iron. Vedantic tradition dates its commencement to the year 3,102 BC, when the warriors of the preceding bronze age destroyed themselves in the cataclysmic battle of Kurukshetra. Virtue has declined to just one quarter. Only truthfulness (or liberality) is widely acknowledged as a natural quality of mankind. The Veda is ignored. Sacrifice falls into disuse and is no longer understood. Disease, lassitude, anger, anguish and fear of scarcity become widespread amongst the population. Natural calamities, such as floods, drought and plagues of rats, locusts and birds occur frequently. All creatures degenerate, their very natures deteriorating. Religious acts produce contrary effects. Men and women neglect their duties. The king oppresses his subjects. *Sudras* become teachers; *Brahmanas* act as servants. Intermixture of the four classes becomes widespread. The voice, pronunciation and minds of men lose their vigour. Diseases become more prevalent. People die prematurely. Cruelty is commonplace. Young girls beget children.

At the beginning of each age there is a relatively short

transitional period called *sandhi*. (A term which, in grammar, refers to the modification of sounds at the conjunction of words.) We are said to be still in the *sandhi* period at the beginning of the iron age. Although people and conditions deteriorate as an age proceeds, the initial *sandhi* period contains in microcosm the nature of the whole following age. Hence we should have a fore-taste now of the worst excesses of the iron age – which is not belied by modern experience of total war, crime, disease, gross immorality, sexual license, greed and so on. Fortunately, we do not lack sustaining examples of truthfulness and liberality that indicate our dependence upon the final leg of virtue.

Transition from bronze age to iron age

At the end of each age evil men appear intent upon destruction. They unwittingly move society towards the precipice of a change from one age to the next. Duryodhana, son of the Kuru king, Dritarashtra, is a prime example from the *Mahabharata*. He is instrumental in bringing about the great war with the Pandus at the end of the age of bronze. Aroused to intense jealousy of his cousins, the Pandu brothers – since they rightly lay claim to the throne of Duryodhana's father – he plans to kill them by building a palace for them, constructed of highly inflammable materials. His plot is foiled when the Pandus are informed of the plot and escape the conflagration by means of a subterranean passage. Subsequently Duryodhana inveigles the eldest Pandu and rightful heir to the throne, Yudhishtira, into a game of dice. Yudhishtira stakes everything, including his wife, Draupadi, and loses. Whereupon Duryodhana rubs salt into the wound by publicly insulting Draupadi, now a slave of the Kurus. He tells his brother, Dussana, to disrobe her in the assembly house before all the lords of the kingdom.

Draupadi, however, is saved from humiliation by her own purity. Some time before she had rescued a *brahmana* from a similar degradation, and this act of kindness now brings divine intervention on her own behalf. As Dussana drags the robes from her body, they are replaced by an endless stream of new ones, hundreds and hundreds, of many hues. At last Dussana falls back, baffled and exhausted.

The wicked Duryodhana undergoes many triumphs and setbacks, until finally, with his army exterminated, he is killed by the mighty king, Bhima. It is then revealed that Duryodhana is no other than Kali himself, the evil man who torments the bull of virtue by cutting off his legs. Yet Yudhishtira, after his own death, is astonished to find Duryodhana seated resplendent in heaven. His acts on earth as a powerful *kshatriya* have earned him celestial rewards. The Pandu king chooses to go to hell to seek the company of his brothers and friends. By doing so he passes the final test of his virtue. Heaven and hell are alike seen as temporary rewards and punishments, which all humans pass through in due measure for their merits and sins on earth. Yudhishtira is at last raised up beyond the celestial worlds 'to enter into the god of righteousness'. For he had adhered to the law of *dharma*. Thus even the terrible descent into the iron age, brought about by the crimes of the warrior class who dominate the age of bronze, is seen ultimately to be no more than the play of *maya*, the illusion of the world, in which men reap the results of their deeds and may, in due time, realize their divine nature.

The *Laws of Manu* confirm the importance attached by the *Mahabharata* to the role of kings in determining the nature, not only of the bronze age, but of every age.

> 'The various ways in which a king behaves resemble the *krita, treta, dvapara,* and *kali* ages; hence the king is identified with the ages of the world. Sleeping he represents the *kali* age, waking the *dvapara*, ready to act the *Treta*, but moving actively the *krita* age.'
>
> (*Laws*, IX, 301–2, p. 396)

For the king stands at the point where the higher knowledge of *Brahman* and of the natural law of *dharma* may pass into the world of human institutions, in the form of religion, education and human laws, to instruct the whole of society. A wise king, advised by *brahmanas*, facilitates this transmission of knowledge; an ignorant king obstructs it. Kingship – or we might broadly say government – is a bridge from the spiritual world to the mundane.

Simultaneity of the four ages

Lest the descriptions of the ages, especially as presented in the violent bronze age drama of the *Mahabharata*, appear far removed from the 'reality' of modern life in the West, some teachers of Vedanta have taught that they may be understood as defining four levels of human life at any instant in history, including the present. All four – golden, silver, bronze and iron – are thus available to whoever chooses to seek them. At any moment life may offer the opportunity to adopt the standpoint of a man or woman of a particular *yuga*. We may 'see the world in a grain of sand', or dismiss it as dirt. We may hear the music of the spheres, or be obsessed with the discordant tumult around us. We may recognize the love ever-present in the person before us, or we may despise their apparent ugliness or faults of character. We may bewail the injustices of our society, or we may see the inherent equity that underlies it. Though we are said to live in the iron age, yet it possesses the characteristics of all four ages, in so far as the *Brahman* and its unmanifest nature is never absent.

The Vedantic doctrine of *karma* can be related to the idea of cycles of time. Since they repeat everlastingly, there is no end within time to the possibility of reincarnation. Each man or woman has lived many lives before, perhaps in all four ages. Like humanity itself, one person rises and falls as his or her *karma* determines. In one embodiment he is a king; in another a beggar. In one embodiment she is a paragon of womanhood; in another a prostitute. Why is it that we each understand so much about lives apparently quite alien to our present one? How do we identify so easily with people from utterly different environments and societies, both in 'real life' and in literature? Perhaps it is because we have been there before, and done that before. Why, too, do we recognize an ideal society, like Plato's Republic, St Augustine's City of God or Thomas More's Utopia; and at the same time can respond to the horrors of Auschwitz or Stalin's slave camps as though we had experienced them? Is it only because we are imaginative or is it because we have witnessed such things in lives beyond this brief passage of seventy years? Once again Vedanta may puzzle our minds with its unfamiliar notions of time, and yet offer a strangely rational explanation for much of what we wrongly take for granted. In so far as any human being – even in the iron age – can come to know *Brahman*, he or she may come to know all things, including the mysteries of time.

> 'And to this day whoever, curbing his interest in external things, knows it, the Brahman ... as "I am *Brahman*", becomes all this, owing to his notion of incompleteness – the effect of ignorance – being removed by the knowledge of *Brahman*. For there is no difference as regards *Brahman*, or the knowledge of it, between giants like Vamadeva [a sage in the *Mahabharata*] and the human weaklings of today. But, one may suppose, the knowledge of *Brahman* may be uncertain in the case of the present generation. This is answered as follows: Even the gods, powerful as they may be, cannot prevail against him, the man who has known *Brahman*.'
>
> (*Brihadaranyaka* Upanishad, I iv 10, p. 111)

Parallels in Western literature

In the Old Testament book of David, King Nebuchadnezzar dreams of an image, whose head is of gold, breast and arms of silver, belly and thighs of brass and legs of iron. A stone smites the image into pieces, which the wind carries away. Daniel interprets the dream to mean that the king is the golden head, and after him shall come inferior kingdoms of silver, brass and iron. But God sets up a kingdom which shall never be destroyed, and from this comes the stone that breaks into pieces the four kingdoms of the earth.

The Greek poet Hesiod was more explicit about the sequence of great ages, though he divided the bronze into two, making five in all. The men of gold 'lived like gods, with carefree hearts, remote from toil and misery'. The earth offered them its fruits of its own accord, and they were beyond all ills and died as if overcome by sleep. In the silver age men lived like children for a hundred years, but then could not restrain themselves from crime, and did not serve the gods with sacrifice. Nevertheless, they were called the 'mortal blessed' and were held in honour by mankind. Bronze age men were, firstly, a terrible and fierce race, with adamantine hearts and misshapen hulks of bodies, and occupied with war and violence. They killed one another and 'went to chill Hades' house of decay, leaving no names'. In the second bronze age they became more righteous and noble, a godly race of heroes, though they too destroyed one another in war. These were the men whom Homer described, who went 'over the great abyss of the sea to Troy on account of lovely-haired Helen'. Some were engulfed by death, but others came to rest in the Isles of the Blessed.

Homer's *Iliad* can be read as a Western counterpart to the battle of Kurukshetra, when the great heroes of the bronze age raged one with another, until most of the values of the age were wiped out. Achilles' smouldering resentment towards Agamemnon, his petulant refusal to fight the Trojans, and his vile treatment of Hector's body are all reminiscent of Duryodhana, as are his magnificent attributes as a warrior. He, too, might have passed through the portals of both heaven and hell, as the result of a career which hastened the collapse of the age of heroes. Certainly it is not difficult to view Homer as depicting a twilight of the gods, marking the end of an era; a time when ancient values of comradeship, magnanimity, hospitality, sacrifice and general nobility of character are giving way to the poverty of vision and feebleness of an iron age.

Yet it is later, in the writings of Plato, that the closest parallels can be found with the historical principles of Vedanta. For him, also, the age in which he lived was a falling off from earlier times.

> 'In the primeval world, and a long while before the cities came into being whose settlements we have described, there is said to have been in the time of Cronos a blessed rule and life, of which the best-ordered of existing states is a copy.'
>
> *(Laws*, IV, s 713, p. 484)

In his *Republic*, Plato develops at length the idea that each man contains, as it were, one of the four metals.

> 'Some of you have the power of command, and in the composition of these he has mingled gold, wherefore also they have the greatest honour; others he has made of silver, to be auxiliaries; others again who are to be husbandmen and craftsmen he has composed of brass and iron; and the species will generally be preserved in the children . . . [but] if the son of a golden or silver parent has an admixture of brass and iron, then nature orders a transposition of ranks . . . just as there may be sons of artisans who having an admixture of gold or silver in them are raised to honour, and become guardians or auxiliaries.'
>
> *(Republic*, III, s 415, pp. 679–80)

Plato regarded the idea that human nature may actually contain any of the four metals as a myth, to be used by the rulers to establish a well ordered society, but he clearly believed that men and women are essentially of four types, which correspond remarkably to the four castes of Vedanta (*see* pp. 203–7). According to the myth, in the iron age especially, parents may give birth to children whose admixture of metal is different from their own, so that the rulers must ensure that means are available for the offspring to find their proper place in society.

In his acknowledgment of Hesiod's insight, and elsewhere in his works, Plato clearly draws upon the idea of succeeding ages, in which the qualities of the rulers deteriorate from gold to iron. His analysis in the *Republic* of the transition of States from aristocracy – the rule of the best; through timocracy – the rule of warriors; oligarchy – the rule of the rich few; democracy – the rule of the *demos* (common people); to a final state of tyranny, when the leader of the poor in their struggle against the rich seizes control on his own account, reflects the decline of the four *yugas*. Plato's timescale is reduced to the level of recorded history. He sees around him, in the wreckage of the Greek *poleis* (city states) caused by the Peloponnesian War, the consequences of rivalry between an arrogant democracy in Athens and a rigid oligarchy in Sparta. His vision of Greek history can be seen as a microcosm of the Vedantic conception of the ineluctable degeneration of the great ages of time.

In later writers, such as Vergil in Rome and Marsilio Ficino in Renaissance Florence, the ancient myth of the four ages is echoed. It is also found outside the field of literature in the collective memory of peoples – amongst the Aboriginals of Australia, the Africans of the Kalahari and the Native Americans of North America, for whom the earth was sacred, as it had been for men of the golden age. Even modern archaeology has strengthened the notion of a bronze age preceding our own epoch, in its discoveries of the shaft tombs of Mycenae and elsewhere, with their accoutrements of heroes, rich in gold.

Conflict with the theory of evolution

The doctrine of the four ages of man appears to be in head-on conflict with Western theories of evolution, based upon the Darwinian principle of natural selection. If Man has evolved from lower forms of life by a process taking millions of years, as most scientists now believe, how can humanity have passed through cycles of time in each of which there is a descent from a golden age towards one of iron? Surely Darwinism, and the mass of observations and theories drawn from many fields of science from geology to molecular biology up to the present day, rule out any possibility that the Vedantic concept of *yugas* is true?

However, whether modern evolutionary theory actually conflicts with Vedanta is not as clear-cut an issue as may appear. Several points have a bearing upon this. Firstly, as the author of the *Encyclopaedia Britannica*'s article on 'Human Evolution' puts it, 'Bitter controversies might have been avoided if a clear distinction had been made between what may be termed anatomical and physiological man and the concept of man in its wider philosophical context'. Vedanta undoubtedly looks at man from the latter point of view. It is not especially concerned with man as a mere physical entity to be found – when dead – as a skeleton or fossil in layers of prehistoric rock. Evolution, whether formulated by Darwin or by modern experts in the workings of DNA, is not about man in the fullest sense, as a creature with physical, mental and spiritual dimensions. Of course, the findings of scientists have a bearing on our understanding of man in a 'wider philosophical context'. They raise difficult questions, such as 'How did man become a creature of mind and spirit?' and 'When did this remarkable transformation happen?' Even these, however, are loaded questions. They assume that the physical entity discovered and analyzed by science became, or was transformed into, something greater than before. Vedanta denies that the consciousness of man ever arose or became anything, since it is eternal and unchanging.

What then is the relationship between the physical man of evolutionary theory and the 'complete' man of Vedanta? Again we must look at the question before trying to answer it. *Brahman* is consciousness. *Brahman* is the sole reality. Therefore it has no relationship with anything. Bodies – whether skeletal or DNA – are contained within consciousness as aspects of *maya*. They do not contain consciousness, as though it were something which leaks away from the skull of a dead hominid. If we do look for a relationship, nevertheless, it is more like that between ink marks on paper and the words they indicate. A scientist might discover everything there is to know about the ink marks – their shape, size, mass, chemical composition, atomic structure, how and when they got there from the past and so on – but if he did not know that they were words, and had meaning, purpose and a part in human life as language, he would have a one-dimensional view of what they 'really' were.

Scientists rely almost exclusively upon empirical evidence. Though they are greatly assisted by instruments, they depend ultimately upon observation by the five senses, mainly those of sight and touch, but the senses are limited to providing information about sense objects. Since man is very much more than a sense object, he cannot be studied by empirical methods alone. Reason, insight and the authority of traditional teachings contribute also to our understanding of humanity.

Nevertheless, in this context, there remains at least one perplexing question about time. Either human life on earth evolved from earlier forms of life and then developed as recognizably man in the relatively short time of about half a million years, or man has lived through numerous *mahayugas*, each of over four million years and each beginning with a golden age. Both cannot be true. Or can they? The Vedantic concept of *karma* may resolve even this dilemma. Historical time for a scientist allows for no recurrence, or reincarnation, of individual men and women. *Karma*, on the contrary, postulates many lives, in each of which the individual experiences the consequences of former ones. These recurring individual lives may relate to the recurring cycles of *yugas*. It may be that we have each lived before in ages of gold, silver, bronze or iron. Perhaps this is why we recognize the poles of love and hatred, beauty and ugliness, harmony and discord, justice and injustice, peace and war. The doctrine of the *yugas* is not an empirical theory. It is not about a one-dimensional line of time. The historical past is a construction based on evidence found in the present, whether of ancient skeletons or of DNA. The *yugas* are not part of that construction; they are part of a creation which includes *karma* and the reincarnation of individuals in another dimension of time.

Yet both the theory of evolution and the doctrine of the four ages are alike unreal when considered in the light of the one final reality of *Brahman*. Time itself – in all its dimensions – is no more than an aspect of *maya*. It is no more real than the 'time' within a dream. Ramana Maharshi draws the parallel:

> 'One sees an edifice in his dream. It rises up all of a sudden. Then he begins to think how it should have been already built brick by brick by so many labourers during such a long time. Yet he does not see the builders working. So also with the theory of evolution. Because he finds himself a man he thinks that he has developed to that stage from the primal state of the amoeba. The man always traces an effect to a cause, there must be a cause for the cause, the argument becomes interminable. Relating the effect to a cause makes the man think. He is finally driven to consider who he is himself.'

> *(Talks, p. 626)*

We may, therefore, believe in both Darwinian evolution and the four *yugas*, each in their own sphere, much as we believe in both ink marks and words. Neither are the final truth. Each helps us to understand features of human life in a limited way. Which one is the more limited is a matter for rational choice.

Chapter 8

Mind

Analysis of mind

A brilliant analogy of the operation of the human mind appears in the *Katha* Upanishad:

> 'Self rides in the chariot of the body, intellect the firm-footed charioteer, discursive mind the reins. Senses are the horses, objects of desire the roads. When Self is joined to body, mind, sense, none but He enjoys. When a man lacks steadiness, unable to control his mind, his senses are unmanageable horses. But if he controls his mind, a steady man, they are manageable horses.'
>
> *(The Ten Principal Upanishads, p. 32)*

The intellect controls actions if the discursive mind, which directs the senses in their pursuit of things that are desired, is obedient to it. But if control is lacking, the senses run wild, like horses that are not reined in.

The *Chandogya* Upanishad gives a fuller and more prosaic analysis of the Vedantic concept of mind. The highest aspect of mind is *chitta*, a word difficult to translate, but approximately equivalent to cognition, understanding or memory in the sense of remembering basic features of life, such as that one is a human being. Perhaps intuition describes *chitta* also, for the *Chandogya* says that it is what enables someone to recognize instantly what something is. It knows the object before words are formulated. Artists have experimented to good effect with 'one glance' pictures, which often show profound features of a subject, rather in the manner of Japanese *haiku* verses. This kind of 'instant knowledge' has been examined in some depth by the American writer Malcolm Gladwell in his recent book *Blink*.

Chitta has also been described as a sort of underlying mental material upon which impressions are made. If it is soft and yielding, the impressions do not last. If it is hard, they make scars, perhaps for life. Hence it has an emotional quality, related to the inherent nature of a person. What kind of life one chooses to lead – one's career, marriage, friends and so on – may be determined by it. Indeed, another important characteristic of *chitta* is determination, the ability to see things through to an end, come what may.

Below *chitta* stands the intellect (*buddhi*). This reasons, discriminates and creates. Reason is essentially concerned with the task of finding the truth. How it operates may be compared with the three kinds of debate or public argument that Vedanta identifies. The lowest form occurs when the protagonists are intent exclusively on the advancement of their own point of view. Somewhat superior to this is the debate in which each rationally opposes the views of his opponent. The highest form, however, is debate in which both parties aim at the truth itself. Only the last exhibits the proper use of reason. Sankara spent much of his short life – he died at the age of thirty-two – in travelling about India debating with opponents, including the growing numbers of Buddhists, in order to spread the purified form of Vedanta to which he had devoted earlier years of study. Many of those whom he defeated in debate and won to his viewpoint are said to have become themselves enthusiastic teachers of *Advaita* Vedanta. In Sankara reason was supreme.

The work of intellect also involves discrimination, defined as the power to choose between reality and unreality, or truth and falsehood. For, like the Roman god, Janus, intellect faces two ways. It looks outwards to the created world, both in its physical and mental aspects, rather like a mirror held up to nature (as Shakespeare describes the art of the theatre); but it also looks back in the opposite direction, inwards towards the self. Hence it can choose between the unreality of the world or the reality of the self, and direct the body and mind, like a charioteer, towards one or the other.

Intellect is, therefore, central to the development of a person's life. For this reason the *Bhagavad Gita*, in particular, looks at intelligence in relation to the three *gunas*. When *sattva* predominates, intellect acts with clarity and speed, without the trace of a doubt. It knows what is real or true or good without hesitation. When *rajas* predominates, intellect begins to doubt. Irresolution creeps in, and decisions may be obscured by feelings like anger or ambition, or alternatively they may be hasty and ill-considered. Intellect dominated by *tamas* becomes muddied and ponderous. Indeed, in this light, reality, truth, goodness and beauty may seem then to be their own opposites. Only the material world is believed to exist. The self is identified with the body. What is good becomes what I desire for myself.

Intellect is also creative. In any field of creative endeavour – art, literature, mathematics, science, politics or law – original work follows upon the clarification of the intellect. Creativity arises not so much from the activity of intellect as from its translucency, for it is informed by the light of the self and draws upon the forms stored in unmanifest nature (*prakriti*). Discursive mind, which controls the senses, may then express what intellect has transmitted to it. Hence the greatest works of art and science, for example, are characterized by clarity and simplicity. This is demonstrably so in Western culture; for instance in ancient Greek sculpture and architecture, the paintings of van Eyck or Vermeer, the stories of Tolstoy, the theorems of Euclid, Newton's laws of motion, the rhetoric of Churchill and the principles of English common law.

Control of the five senses is a major function of discursive mind (*manas*). It receives impressions from without, organizes them and offers them, as it were, to intellect. This role as a kind of servant is easily abused. If not guided by intellect, the charioteer holding the reins of *manas*, control over the senses becomes disordered. They may run riot in excesses of greed or even of unnecessary austerity; they may become intermixed, so that the senses of touch or sight, for example, subvert the sense of hearing. People can become obsessed with one sense, so that the others are atrophied.

Discursive mind, however, has other functions. It deals with information of all kinds. Ordinary experience consists largely of receiving, sorting out and storing factual material – things, events, times and places. *Manas* is the Bradshaw or railway timetable of the mind. It tells us what services are running, when, where and how. Thus it is a human computer, stocked with records, continually receiving information and making it available when required; yet *manas* is utterly dependent on an intelligent operator and is in itself devoid of reason, discrimination and creativity.

These are the three great 'organs' of mind for Vedanta. Strictly they are not organs at all; they are purely functions of mind, known collectively as *antahkarana* (the internal organ). What then is mind? Its material cause – what it is made of – is said to be the subtle elements of space, air, fire, water and earth. This is not so strange if we consider once more the dream world – itself often called the mental realm. Dreams and imaginings are made of such subtle materials as imagined space and fire (colours). There is, of course, mental activity not obviously consisting of such sense images, but of what are such imageless thoughts made? Do we not hear them with an 'inner ear'? If so, they are made of ether (subtle space) as the ground of audibility. In the general order of creation, from *Brahman* to the element of earth, mind appears as ego, but constituted of the subtle forms of the five elements. Ramana Maharsi develops further implications of this idea of mind as ego (*see* pp. 154–5).

Mind is an elusive concept, both in Vedanta and in Western philosophy. The Upanishads use the idea of attention to confirm that mind does indeed exist. If there were only the self, the senses and their objects, with no intermediate mind, then how, they argue, can we sometimes be aware of a sense object, like a sound, and sometimes not be aware of the same sound even when it is continuous? Either the self and the sense would always be connected with the sound, or they would never be connected. In fact, the same sound 'comes and goes'. For example, as I write this I hear a clock ticking. A few moments ago I did not. Why? Obviously I was not attending to it before. The mind was attending to something else. The self and sense of hearing did nothing. Mind, therefore, controls attention, or directs consciousness into particular channels.

The *Chandogya* Upanishad does not analyze mind into just the three components of *chitta*, intellect and discursive mind, though elsewhere in Vedanta they are taken to be the essential ones. Between *chitta* and intellect it places resolution (*samkalpa*). This is the power to establish an aim or purpose. Any human action involves such a resolution. Most are minor issues, like a resolution to get up or sit down. Some are major directions for life, like the choice of a career. Resolutions are good or bad. The former are conducive to self-realization, the latter are not. However, beyond both of these are resolutions which have no personal end in view at all. They lead to actions taken purely for the sake of *Brahman*, with no purpose intended for oneself or others. A mark of such actions is the degree of attention given to them. When total attention is given to the action itself, then the actor serves *Brahman* alone. In the *Bhagavad Gita*, Krishna instructs Arjuna to act in this way; to make himself an instrument in the hands of *Brahman* and to forget all his doubts about the morality of killing his own relatives on the battlefield.

> 'He [the sage] offers *Brahman* everything he does.
> From every taint of sin he lives immune,
> Like lotus leaves upon the water's brim.'
>
> (*Bhagavad Gita*, V, 9–10, p. 64)

Above *chitta* the *Chandogya* places meditation. This may be
understood as a means of transcending mind altogether. It
requires, however, the mental act or function of attention being
concentrated upon a mantra, such as the sound *OM*, until
persistent practice leads finally to union with the self or *Brahman*.
Obviously meditation is not an ordinary habitual function of mind;
it is a consciously chosen means of self-realization, requiring
instruction into a traditional mantra. The *Mandukya* Upanishad
compares it to the art of archery.

> 'Om is the bow; the soul is the arrow; and Brahman is
> called its target. It is to be hit by an unerring man. One
> should become one with It just like an arrow.'
> (*Mandukya* Upanishad, II ii 4, in *The Eight Upanishads*,
> Vol. 2, p. 132)

According to Sankara, only he 'who is unerring, who is free from
the errors of desiring to enjoy external objects, who is detached
from everything, who has control over his senses and has concentration of mind' should shoot at the target of *Brahman*. *OM* is the
bow; the personal self is the arrow. Through the practice of meditation the personal self is carried, by the force of the mantra *OM*,
towards union with the universal self. Elsewhere Sankara describes
meditation as withdrawing the senses into *manas*, *manas* into
buddhi and then contemplating the *Brahman* in *buddhi*, until all
separation has fallen away, a process 'like a line of flowing oil'.

Such a simple analysis of mind into a few basic functions may
appear naïve and unscientific, particularly to Western philosophers
and psychologists. For this reason it is worth quoting a perceptive
remark Wittgenstein made about modern psychology as a discipline.

> 'The confusion and barrenness of psychology is not to be
> explained by calling it a "young science"; . . . in psychology
> there are experimental methods and *conceptual confusion*.'
> (*Philosophical Investigations*, p. 197)

The conceptual simplicity of the analysis of mind in Vedanta could help to create a more mature science of psychology in the West.

Control of mind

The nature of the mind is to be in continual movement. Thoughts, feelings, images and dreams pass through it, like clouds driven by the wind. Hence it is hard to control, as Arjuna complains to Krishna:

> 'Sooner harness the tempestuous wind
> Than with the steady yoga you commend
> Restrain for long the restless, forceful mind,
> So turbulent, so quick, so unconfined!'
> *(Bhagavad Gita*, VI, 33–4, p. 70)

But restraint is not impossible, replies his master. Practice is needed, such as continuous reflection on an idea of *Brahman*, perhaps in the form of a word or image. Ramana Maharshi has the very same message:

> 'The mind is by nature restless. Begin liberating it from its restlessness; give it peace; make it free from distractions; train it to look inward; make this a habit. This is done by ignoring the external world and removing the obstacles to peace of mind.'
> *(Talks*, p. 27)

Much of the practice of Vedanta, as opposed to its theory, involves exercises of this kind. For the mind is the arena of philosophy as a practical study. On one side self remains ever unmoved and serene; on the other the body operates under natural laws of anatomy and physiology, which need no correction nor interference, except where illness or injury require the intervention of medical science. But in between self and body lies the unceasing movement of mind. Here are the ideas that determine a man or woman's life, that govern choice, mould the future, create *karma* for lives to come. In mind, and only in mind, can philosophy itself bring to one's life a profound change. Only here can one choose – as a Sanskrit prayer puts it – between non-being or being, darkness or light, death or immortality.

To attempt to change the nature of the mind, to force it to stop moving or to drive out any of its contents, is futile, as Arjuna had observed. Only by surrendering it completely to *Brahman* can it be finally controlled. What then is this 'giving up' of the mind? What is left of, or in, the mind when it has been surrendered? Vedanta describes in a variety of ways the condition of the sage who has transcended mind. Sometimes transcendence of mind is regarded as leaving it largely unchanged, but without any attachment to it or its contents on the part of the realized man. He is indifferent to its processes. He views them as one watching the passing clouds in the sky. Ideas, emotions, pleasures, pains hold no hopes or fears for him. They do not touch him, for he is at one with *Brahman*, the sole reality. How can he be moved by shadows that flicker on a wall, like those in Plato's cave? Sometimes mind is seen as itself becoming quiescent, as though reflecting the serenity of the self rather than the commotion of the world. Such a view emphasises the quality of *sattva*, which permeates the mind of the sage, though he is indifferent even to this.

The most radical conclusion is that the mind of the sage ceases to exist. He literally becomes mindless. Although Sankara occasionally seems to hold this view, it is developed more extensively by Ramana Maharshi, in accordance with his idiosyncratic teaching on the subject of mind. For him, mind is nothing more than the sum total of the thoughts that it contains. The central thought, however, that acts like a keystone in the arch of mind, is the thought of 'I', namely the ego. If ego is sustained, so are all thoughts; if ego is removed, the whole edifice of thoughts comes crashing down with it. Hence, time and again, Maharshi asserts the need to weaken and destroy the ego; to go behind it to its source, which is the real self, so that it can be seen for what it is, an imposter, a false self masquerading as the real one. Often when a student brought a question about his philosophical difficulties – intellectual or otherwise – the master would undercut the question with one of his own: Who has this problem? Seek out the questioner, find the source of him, not of his problem. Then the problem disappears with him, for he is the ego. Do you have this problem when you are asleep? But you exist when you are asleep. The ego finds that it has the question when you wake up. Then stay with the one who sleeps. Forget the one who questions.

> 'The mind is only a bundle of thoughts. The thoughts arise because there is the thinker. The thinker is the ego. The ego, if sought, will vanish automatically. The ego and the mind are the same. The ego is the root-thought from which all other thoughts arise.'
>
> (*Talks*, p. 166)

> 'A spurious "I" arises between the pure consciousness and the insentient body and imagines itself limited to the body. Seek this and it will vanish as a phantom. That phantom is the ego, or the mind of the individuality.'
>
> (*Talks*, p. 413)

It follows from such an approach that, if the ego really is destroyed, then there are no thoughts and hence no mind. Does this degree of fundamentalism make sense? Again Maharshi might answer that it makes no sense at all to the ego, but perfect sense to the self. The self is consciousness. The personal mind is merely a means of directing the consciousness of an individual. When the individual is merged in the universal *Brahman* 'his' consciousness is everywhere. How can it need to be directed? As the *Gita* puts it: What need for water tanks if there is a flood? Self, senses and body act as one for the realized man. His attention does not flicker on and off with every twist of the mind.

'Yet who restrains
Each from their object, every wilful sense,
His knowledge is most firm, O Arjuna.
For such a one, what all men call the night
Is when he wakes; whilst when they wake is what
He calls the night. There is no peace for him
Who wants desire, but when, as rivers flow
And fill the tranquil ocean from all sides,
Desires flow into him, that man finds peace,
Longing for nothing, giving up desire,
Without a sense of "I" or what is "mine";
O son of Pritha, that is peace indeed.'

(*Bhagavad Gita*, II, 68–71, p. 52)

An alternative view of the condition of the realized man is that the personal, or individual, mind becomes merged into universal mind. The latter concept is not widely found in Vedanta. Its Sanskrit name is *Hiranyagarbha*, meaning the golden foetus, since it is associated with the golden egg from which, in some Vedantic creation myths, the universe is born. It is also identified with *Brahma*, the creator god. The relationship of *Hiranyagarbha* to the physical world is that of the individual mind to the body. Hence it possesses universal will and power of organization, with functions that correspond to those of memory, intellect and discursive mind. However, on a universal level these functions are regarded as pure, and do not exhibit the negative features, or evil tendencies, found in the minds of individuals. For this reason the realized man, whose life is controlled by universal mind, always adheres to the path of *dharma*, the law of righteousness.

In the West, particularly in the 18th century, the argument from design for the existence of God also employed the notion of a universal mind. Newton's discovery of the laws of gravity and planetary motion and other advances in science suggested that the universe exhibited perfect order and rationality. Such a grand design was thought to prove the existence of an intelligent and beneficent God. Universal mind was the instrument of God to achieve this design, an intermediary, as in the individual human, between self and body.

Mind and reincarnation

How is the Vedantic concept of mind related to reincarnation? The real self, the *Atman* which is identical with *Brahman*, is not reincarnated, for it is not created in the first place. It is immutable. Likewise, an individual self does not reincarnate for there is no individual self apart from the universal self. In the mind of the individual exists a belief that they are different, but in reality they are the same. Hence there can be no reincarnation of an individual self. Then is the individual body reincarnated, or as a Christian would say, resurrected? Vedanta denies this also. Each body is unique. In one lifetime a man or woman has one body, its form at birth determined by *karma* inherited from previous embodiments and modified by the life led subsequently. Later lifetimes of the same person are lived in new bodies, themselves products of *karma*.

So what is reincarnated? Who or what is the person appearing in body after body? Mind alone remains as the 'material' from which a reincarnated person can be constructed. At death the mental tendencies accumulated from previous lives, including the last one of the dying man, are not destroyed. The physical elements of the body revert to their universal counterparts – earth to earth, and so on – as stated in the Christian burial service. The mental or subtle elements are preserved to enter another body in another life – hence the crucial importance of the dominant thought at the moment of death. Shantanand Saraswati also emphasizes the company that the person chose to keep when alive:

> 'It is true that the individual, in ignorance, is attached to coarser levels in place of finer, and this is why he keeps on coming back to the physical form birth after birth. This is part of the laws of nature. The sort of company one

keeps is the sort of company to which nature will return you. When a person dies in ignorance he goes to the finer, or subtle level, but very soon comes back to the coarse level he was used to. The laws of nature will compel him to turn back to the coarse level and pay the price for his comfortable attachments. This is the cycle which is being repeated all the time. But this vicious circle of birth, death and birth can be broken.'

(*Birth and Death*, p. 35)

He goes on to compare birth and death to waking and sleeping. When we go to sleep we more or less leave the physical world and enter the dream world. Then we awake and revert to the physical world in our waking state. Likewise, when we die we leave the physical world, but 'keep all the knowledge which is the element of the subtle world'. The subtle 'body' gets reborn with a new physical form and carries on with the knowledge and ingrained tendencies that together constitute its *karma*. This continuity of knowledge is a vital fact. The *Bhagavad Gita* says that no effort, however small, to realize the self can ever be lost. Thus whatever knowledge of *Brahman*, or how to unite with it, is gained in a particular lifetime is always retained to become available in future lives.

An objection presents itself here. Is it just the mind that experiences life after life? If so, then there is really no person, no complete human being with a spiritual nature, there at all. Reincarnation would not then be an explanation of human destiny, but merely an account of how a human mind alone undergoes a series of reincarnations. Has the soul or spirit been lost in all this? Vedanta's answer is clearly 'No'. The *jiva*, the individual aspect of the one eternal *Brahman*, is also present in the reincarnated person, even though not itself embodied. As *Brahman* it does not come and go with each birth and death. Just as the *jiva* remains unchanged throughout the three states of waking, dream and sleep, so it is immutable when the mind undergoes cycles of birth and death. When the mind enters a new body, it carries with it a belief in separation. It contains the belief in the separation of 'its own' spirit from the universal spirit. A human being as a physical and psychic creature is an embodiment of *Brahman*. In spirit it is *Brahman* and nothing else at all. But the mind goes on believing in individuality. This is the one cardinal mistake that is responsible for embodiment in the first place. When the mistake is recognized and eliminated, then there are no more lives to be experienced. The *jiva* is freed from its apparent limitations and 'unites' with the *Brahman*, from which it was never really separate.

This is why the mind is the battlefield, the place where the struggle to rid oneself of false ideas must be undergone. The *Chandogya* makes this explicit.

> 'Because a person is identified with his conviction, there-
> fore just as the conviction a man has in this world, so does
> he become after departure from here. Therefore he should
> shape his conviction.'
>
> (*Chandogya* Upanishad, III 13 8, p. 208)

The conviction that 'I am so and so, a person of a certain type and character' needs to be replaced with the simple truth that 'I am *Brahman*'. Only then do the cycles of reincarnation, the endless succession of lives – or as Vedanta sometimes terms them, 'the misery of existence' – come to an end. Like the donkeys who thought they were tethered, and stayed still all night long in that belief, we only need to release ourselves from false ideas. Mind alone is the secret of bondage and of freedom.

Mind/body dualism

The famous problem in philosophy of how body and mind are related does not seem to have gained a foothold in Vedanta. Western philosophers, especially since Descartes, have been beset by the belief, in one form or another, that body and mind are two distinct substances. How then can they interact? How can the state of the body affect the mind, as in the case of pleasure and pain? And how can the mind be brought to bear on the body, as appears to happen with, for example, decisions to act? In its modern form the problem appears devoid of the classical and medieval concept of substance, but it remains equally puzzling. How is it that my arm rises, when in my mind I make a decision to raise it? Does a physiologist fall short of the truth when he explains the movement entirely by physical conditions? And so on.

If the problem is couched in terms of substance, Vedanta has the simplest possible answer. There is only one substance, namely consciousness. Everything is consciousness – physical things, such as bones, muscles and nerves, and also mental phenomena, such as thoughts, desires and emotions. Hence there is no conceivable problem of relating one substance to another. Bodies are spatial – they are comprised of space, plus the other four elements. Thoughts are non-spatial – their 'material' is the subtle elements, including ether, which is the subtle space in which they are heard internally. As Kant might have said, physical things exist in outer sense and mental things in inner sense. Both inner and outer sense contain representations, which all occur under the conditions of both empirical and transcendental unity of apperception. Or, as Vedanta says, the material world is the waking state of awareness of spatial objects, while the mental world is the dream state of awareness of mental functions. Kant's empirical unity of apperception is the apparent unity of mind in the ego, and his transcendental unity can be understood as the real unity of everything in *Brahman*.

But does the mind/body problem go away so easily? A modern philosopher gives a neat example of its continued potency.

> 'If a scientist took off the top of your skull and looked into your brain while you were eating a chocolate bar, all he would see is a grey mass of neurons. If he used instru-

ments to measure what was happening inside, he would
detect complicated physical processes of many different
kinds. But would he find the taste of chocolate?'

(What Does It All Mean?, p. 29)

Surely there is an irreducible gulf between neurons and the like,
and the subjective taste of chocolate? How can Vedanta bridge
that? A later quote from the same author gives a clue.

'There seem to be two very different kinds of things going
on in the world: the things that belong to physical reality,
which many different people can observe from the outside,
and those other things that belong to mental reality, which
each of us experiences from the inside in his own case.'

(What Does It All Mean?, p. 36)

The last four words, seemingly innocuous, are most significant.
Ordinarily we would never question them. When I am eating chocolate surely the taste of it is peculiar to me. It is my own case and
no one else's. We all have our own particular taste of chocolate.
However, behind the language lurks the strongly held belief that
I am ultimately – one might say metaphysically – separate from
others. My awareness of the taste of chocolate is therefore uniquely
mine. Yet the frailty of this belief is revealed when it is expressed
as a mere tautology. 'My taste of chocolate is mine.' Well, of course;
it would be a verbal contradiction to say that mine was his or hers.
As Wittgenstein explained, I might point forcibly to myself as I say
it, but how can such body language elucidate a tautology? It merely
shows how powerful is my conviction that I am indeed a separate
entity, that consciousness somehow belongs to me especially, or
at least a little bit of it does.

But I do not have to 'shape my conviction' in that way. Such an
example illustrates how Vedanta deals with such problems by
attempting to uproot ideas that are fundamental, yet false.
Consciousness is one. It has no bits. It is not partly mine and partly

someone else's. No sense can be made of a special taste logically unique to the individual. There are no logically private worlds in which we each live. There is only one world, and we all live in that same one.

While each person has one body and one mind, these are no more than individual instances of universal 'materials' available to all. To say 'But only I can know what is going on in my mind.' is exactly akin to saying 'Only I can see what is happening now across the street.' If you were there, you would see the same thing. If you had my thoughts now, you would think the same things as I am thinking. The word 'same' is ambiguous (*see* p. 46). Mental 'objects', like thoughts, can be of the same kind, but they cannot be represented as the very same ones, even to the person who has them. Such an analysis is in keeping with the principles of Vedanta. Sages in the tradition of *Advaita* have probably ignored such problems, because they could not believe that anyone would be so obtuse as to believe in logically separate individual minds or private worlds.

Other minds

The problem of the existence of other minds is also stated very clearly by Nagel.

> 'The only example you've ever directly observed of a correlation between mind, behaviour, anatomy, and physical circumstances is yourself. Even if other people and animals had no experiences whatever, no mental inner life of any kind, but were just elaborate biological machines, they would look just the same to you. So how do you know that's not what they are? How do you know that the beings around you aren't all mindless robots? You've never seen into their minds – you couldn't – and their physical behaviour could all be produced by purely physical causes. Maybe your relatives, your neighbors, your cat and your dog have *no inner experiences whatever*. If they don't, there is no way you could ever find it out.'
>
> (*What Does It All Mean?*, p. 23)

Once again the straightforward answer of Vedanta is to point to the one consciousness of *Brahman*, of which all individual minds are no more than a manifestation. Hence I, the real self, know everything about every mind, and it is only the ego that says to itself, 'I only have knowledge of one mind, namely my own, and therefore can only observe one correlation between mind and behaviour.' How could this ego be aware directly of other minds, any more than this body could carry out the actions of other people? Therefore the only correlation between mind and body that can be observed by one person as the ego is that between his or her own mind and his or her own body.

To a Western philosopher this seems to raise more problems than it solves. Firstly, in what sense can I know everything about all minds? Surely I only know about other minds by inference, analogy and by what other people tell me, if indeed I know anything at all about them? Such an argument forces the Vedantist to explain what is meant by observation by the real self. One answer to this is to ask once more whether one exists in deep sleep and, if so, how does one know this? Vedanta affirms that we do so exist and, moreover, that we recognize this when we are awake. How did we know? Only by a kind of observation or consciousness which lies beyond or behind the awareness of the waking state. That consciousness is what knows also about other minds, though it does not usually pass this knowledge on to the ego. For this reason we do not seriously doubt the existence of other minds, even if we may imagine a doubt.

A second problem for Vedanta is that *Brahman*, the one real self, does not seem to 'directly observe correlations' of any kind. It does, indeed, observe, but to observe correlations requires some mental activity also. Here the Vedantist can turn the argument back on itself. Who said that we only know of other minds by means of correlations? Of course, modern philosophers say it; no one else! When you meet a stranger do you extrapolate from your own observed correlations between body and mind, and then conclude that he or she has a mind? Or do you just smile, say hello, and carry on, at least as though he or she has one? Clearly, we believe straight away that any human being has a mind. We do this because something 'in us' – perhaps consciousness – tells us that there is a mind there. Perhaps *chitta*, or memory, plays a part, but the real knowledge comes from the self, which knows that it – the self – is universal. Naturally we are all one, but we learn by false education to believe that we are many. Vedanta takes on the task of undoing this belief. Yet when we meet a stranger and immediately say 'hello', we have achieved in an instant what Vedanta would teach. Do we say 'hello' to a table? As Winston Churchill insisted, when told as a small boy to learn the vocative of *mensa*, he did not address tables. We recognize the consciousness of the one self in others as directly as we recognize it in ourselves.

> 'For the self is not a thing unknown to anybody at any time, is not a thing to be reached or got rid of or acquired ... Wherefore, just as there is no need for an external evidence by which to know one's own body, so there is no need for an external evidence by which to know the self who is even nearer than the body.'
>
> (*Bhagavad Gita*, Sankara's commentary, p. 489)

Chapter 9

Theism and Dualism

Advaita Vedanta has been the dominant form of Vedanta, particularly through the influence of Sankara in the early Middle Ages. However, another form, less developed philosophically but more potent in terms of religious belief in India, has been the *bhakti yoga*, or way of devotion, expounded by Ramanuja in the 12th century AD. Sankara himself acknowledged that devotion as an aspect of philosophy could be traced back to the Upanishads, indeed to the Rig Veda, in which Vishnu is a great sky god, later to become the one god especially associated with this branch of Vedanta. Yet for Sankara devotion was one of the three ways of attaining self-realization, rather than the philosophical basis for religion. The other two ways were the way of action (*karma yoga*) and the way of knowledge (*jnana yoga*). All three appear in the *Bhagavad Gita*, and Sankara emphasized that, particularly for the householder, all three could be practised together. Thus *Advaita* Vedanta sees the way of devotion as an integral part of the *Advaita* system, and not as an alternative form of Vedanta itself.

Ramanuja saw himself as in the tradition of the way of devotion, but for him it was especially associated with Vishnu and the religious movement known as Vaisnavism, which had spread throughout India, notably in the south, since about the 1st century BC. Nevertheless Ramanuja was a philosopher of Vedanta. He travelled widely as a teacher and wrote significant commentaries on the Upanishads, the *Bhagavad Gita* and the *Brahma Sutra*.

Above all, Ramanuja denied the whole doctrine of *maya* and the idea that the world is an illusion. For him reality is not unitary but threefold. *Brahman* (which he identified with Vishnu), souls and matter are all real. All three indeed are eternal. How then can he be considered to be a Vedantist at all? The answer is that he regarded *Brahman* as the only independent reality, possessed of *sat* – pure, absolute, independent existence. Souls and matter are utterly dependent upon *Brahman*. They could not exist without it. *Brahman* is their efficient cause; it alone offers souls a purpose and a goal; and it creates the system of *karma* which governs the cycle of lives for each soul. Every soul and material thing is a part of *Brahman*, a finite – if eternal – fraction of the one independent reality. Yet Ramanuja asserts that *Brahman* is indivisible. How then can it have parts? The parts are attributes of *Brahman*, related as qualities to its substance. Unlike Sankara's *Brahman*, in which there is no distinction of substance and quality, Ramanuja's has distinct qualities, which are infinite, though containing finite members in the form of souls and material things.

These souls belong to animals and plants, as well as to men and, indeed, gods. They are real and eternal, but lack three characteristics possessed by *Brahman*: firstly, independence; secondly, infinite size (for they are atomic); and, thirdly, the power to create. Souls fall into several types. The souls of gods are always in the company of *Brahman*, united with him as devotees, but not identical to him. The souls of other creatures, notably men, include those who have won freedom from embodiment in the world by their own efforts to transcend their *karma*, and those whose attachment to the world compels them to continued participation in the cycles of *karma*. Ramanuja attaches much importance to the responsibility of each soul for the creation of its own *karma*, while he insists on the ultimate sovereignty of *Brahman* in creating the laws that govern what is due to each individual soul. Freed souls lose all distinctions associated with the material world, yet they retain their individuality for ever, existing merely to contemplate the divine glory of *Brahman*.

Ramanuja's teaching is usually called 'qualified *Advaita*' or theism. The latter title emphasizes the primacy of Vishnu and the doctrine of the one supreme god. Even Brahma, the creator god, and Siva, the destroyer, merge in Vishnu, who no longer acts as the mere sustaining divinity of the universe. The former title emphasizes that Ramanuja does not indulge in duality, or a plurality of absolute beings, but retains a belief in one fundamental, independent *Brahman*. His critics, of course, ask how *Advaita* can be qualified at all. Does qualification amount to some loss of the unlimited, total reality of the one *Brahman*? Ramanuja's answer to this was to interpret the apparently unqualified monism of the Veda and other scriptures in his own way. 'That thou art', 'I am *Brahman*' and other cardinal statements of non-dualism, he saw as assertions of the complete dependence of souls and matter upon God. Without God, nothing, no existence, no souls, no matter. For the world, he said, is the body of God. Thus God is also the material cause of everything.

Ramanuja also had positive arguments against unqualified *Advaita* Vedanta. Identity as a concept, he argued, depends upon difference (and vice versa). If there is no conceivable difference between anything, then the concept of the identity of anything – *Brahman*, in particular – makes no sense. Sankara did not ignore this problem. For him, the real identity of *Brahman* and the individual self (*jiva*) is in contradistinction to their apparent duality. *Brahman* and *jiva* seem to be separate, but in reality they are one. Ramanuja's defence was that identity and difference must both be used of reality; hence *Brahman* and *jiva* are really different – and yet also really identical in the special sense of the complete dependence of *jiva*.

A second point made by Ramanuja concerns Sankara's concept of reality. For Sankara anything which comes and goes is not real. In other words, any real thing is permanent; its existence is not subject to time. This means, of course, that nothing in creation is

real. Only *Brahman* satisfies this severe criterion of reality.
Ramanuja criticizes this with the following argument. Nothing can
exist and not exist at the same time. But something can exist and
not exist at different times. Hence the concept of existence does
not require that what exists has to exist always. Since he assumes
that Sankara uses a concept of existence that does require this, he
regards Sankara's conclusion about reality to be false. In fact,
Sankara probably relied on the kind of analysis of existence used
by Plato; namely that being must be distinguished from becoming,
so that whereas all things in the world are in a condition of
becoming, only *Brahman* has being, as opposed to becoming. In
his *Gita* commentary, for example, Sankara uses the concept of
sat, or being, in the same way that Ramanuja himself uses it to
refer to *Brahman* – to mean absolute, immutable, totally independent existence. For Ramanuja to deny any distinction between
being and becoming is tantamount to denying the distinction
between reality and illusion, which, of course, he does deny. This,
perhaps, leaves the argument to be resolved by other means.

Thirdly, Ramanuja attacked Sankara's concept of ignorance,
perhaps the most difficult point in the latter's thought. The individual self before realization is beset by ignorance of the truth that
it is one with the universal self. Dispelling ignorance is the task of
philosophy. Yet whose ignorance is it? It cannot belong to the
Brahman, whose very nature is *sat–chit–ananda*. Nor can it really
belong to the individual self, for if it did the self could not free
itself from it – in other words, if ignorance were an aspect of its
nature, it would have to change its nature. But the individual self,
even while apparently ignorant, is already at one with Brahman
and the nature of *Brahman*. Hence ignorance belongs to nobody!
Ramanuja was well aware of this problem for *Advaita* generally. It
was less of a problem for him, because he believed that the individual soul *becomes* free (but is not free already) and hence can
rid itself of its ignorance.

Ramana Maharshi dealt with this criticism quickly enough.
When a questioner asked him to whom ignorance belonged, he

replied simply, 'To you, the questioner!' Sankara himself, in his *Gita* commentary, says that ignorance arises in the unmanifest nature and gives rise to the ego, which suggests that ignorance is not so much removed from the individual as transcended. Moreover, unlike Ramanuja, Sankara regards individuality as illusory; hence he can argue that the individual aspect of nature – the ignorance which is the seed of ego – does not really exist. Why then bother about the question of to whom ignorance belongs?

In Vedantic terms, Ramanuja can be understood to deny the existence of *Nirguna Brahman* and claim that there is only *Saguna Brahman*. His theory of knowledge confirms this, since he asserted that all knowledge involves a subject and object. Hence the absolute unity of *Nirguna Brahman*, in which there is only consciousness with no object which it knows, becomes meaningless. This, of course, conforms to his denial of the absolute union of souls with *Brahman*, for the freed souls remain as individuals, which know *Brahman* as an object. Their everlasting contemplation of *Brahman* is, indeed, the whole rationale of their continued existence.

Advaita Vedanta, on the other hand, regards the idea of eternal individual souls as quite unsatisfactory. In what sense are they distinct individuals, since they have no distinctive features of any kind? Men, animals, plants and gods remain permanently as individuals, and yet are descriptively the same, each with a merely numerical identity of its own. Ramanuja's view is that freed souls have lost the ego, but have retained individuality. *Advaita*, on the contrary, sees this as confusing the soul (*jiva*) with the ego. It is the latter which gives rise in the first place to the very notion of individuality. When it has been lost, or transcended, there is no individuality, and the *jiva* realizes that it is in truth nothing other than *Brahman*.

The way of devotion

It is easy to see how Ramanuja's philosophical standpoint relates to the way of devotion. Since the world is the body of God, everything in the world is to be loved as God. A story illustrates this point. There was a saint, called Eknath, who set off from the source of the Ganges, at Gangotri in the Himalayas, to take some of its holy water some 2,000 miles to a temple known as Rameshwaram at Land's End in southern India. On the way he came across a donkey lying in the road, almost dead from thirst. Eknath stopped and poured all the holy water down the donkey's throat. The donkey soon sprang up and walked away. Eknath prayed to Siva, the god of Rameshwaram. 'I was asked by you to fetch holy water for you from Gangotri, but fortunately you have just met me on the way, so I have happily performed the duty.' The voice of Siva came to him to honour his act of devotion.

On the way of devotion the devotee does not make plans or prepare in advance for his meeting with God. He finds God anywhere and everywhere. Nor is he interested in *Nirguna Brahman*. An abstract God, without qualities, is of no concern to him. The world around him contains God in every person or creature or particle. For this reason a devotee can easily pray to or worship an idol, like a stone statue, for he sees God in it. Obviously such a viewpoint lends itself to abuse, so that the worship of stone statues may become idolatry, but the true devotee does not make this mistake. *Brahman* is not matter; yet *Brahman* is found in matter. The world is the body of God. However, the modern Indian philosopher, Radhakrishnan, has criticized this aspect of theism. If *Brahman* has a spiritual 'soul' of its own and a body – the world – how can it be one and indivisible? As he says, you cannot cook half a chicken and expect the other half to lay eggs!

The word *bhakti*, meaning devotion, worship and faith, connotes also division or separation. Indeed, the concept of devotion surely implies an act or attitude of a person to something else, whether it is *Brahman*, God, another person or an idol. The very concept is dualistic. It is not surprising, therefore, that *bhakti yoga*, or the way of devotion, has become much associated with religion, and particularly with Hinduism. Ramanuja has provided a philosophical structure for many Hindus. Some teachers of

Advaita Vedanta, on the other hand, have given devotion a non-dualistic meaning. How is this possible?

Devotion in *Advaita* Vedanta

One answer is given in the *Bhagavad Gita*, since it contains all three ways to self-realization: those of action, devotion and knowledge. The section on devotion describes how Krishna – who for Vaisnavism is an incarnation of Vishnu – reveals to Arjuna his divine form. In place of a *kashtriya* charioteer there suddenly appears a magnificent, terrifying and overwhelming vision of God as the divine force of the whole world.

> 'In your own body, Lord, I see the gods,
> And hosts of creatures, every kind of thing:
> The Lord *Brahma* upon his lotus seat,
> The seers of old and serpents of the skies.
> I see you, Lord, so infinite in form;
> On every side I see your myriad arms,
> Your bellies, mouths and eyes; there is no end,
> No place where you begin, nor one between.
> O Lord of every form, O Lord Supreme,
> Adorned with crowns, with club and discus armed,
> A radiant mass of universal light,
> Of blazing fire and bright effulgent Suns,
> My eyes can barely see your boundless might.
> (*Bhagavad Gita*, XI, 15–17, p. 93–4)

The Sun and Moon become the eyes of God, space becomes his body, in his mouth burn fires that consume all things at the end of time; yet the world is warmed by the benevolence of his face. He is the Alpha and Omega of all that exists, infinite in power, worthy of all praise. Arjuna has seen *Saguna Brahman*, shorn of all its familiar and habitual associations, the immanence of God as an immediate presence. Unhinged by this cataclysmic experience, Arjuna cries out for Krishna to appear once more as his charioteer, his beloved friend and adviser. The relative normality of the battlefield is restored, but Arjuna henceforth is utterly devoted to Krishna, the incarnation of God whom he now knows for certain as the Lord of all.

Wary of another step into the abyss of the unknown, Arjuna asks Krishna whether it is better to seek the unmanifest *Nirguna Brahman* or to worship him, Krishna, the *Brahman* incarnate. Krishna's wise advice is that to seek the One immovable, outside of time, beyond all definition and all thought, is a hard task and greater trouble than to worship and serve him, Krishna, the friend whose love extends to every creature and is ever available. He goes on to enumerate the practices on the way of devotion or love: to offer all actions to him, to meditate on him alone, to set the mind on union with him, to cast aside the fruits of action, to renounce all gain, to be compassionate, patient and contented, to remain unmoved by pleasure and pain, undisturbed by the clamour of the world, to depend upon no one, covet nothing, rise above good and evil, to be free from attachment, to follow *dharma* – the eternal law. Such a one, Krishna repeats, is especially dear to him, the highest in his esteem. Yet on this interpretation of the *Gita*, the final goal is union with Krishna, not perpetual adoration of him.

A story illustrates how complete dedication brings final release. However great the obstacles, faith and determination will eventually bring their reward. Two birds had a nest on a rock by the sea. One day some high waves washed away their eggs. The birds were determined to punish the sea for its cruelty and to recover their eggs. They began to pick up grains of sand in their beaks and deposit them in the sea; then to return with drops of seawater to leave on the shore. Each day they worked at this task unremittingly. A passing saint observed their strange behaviour and enquired about it. 'We are absolutely determined to fill up the sea with sand', the birds explained. 'Even if it takes many lifetimes, we will continue until the task is completed.' The saint was so impressed by their resolution and faith that he decided to help them. He had miraculous powers, which could dry up the sea. When he threatened to do this if the eggs were not returned, the sea was afraid and brought the eggs back to the nest.

Another reading of the *Gita*, advocated by Sankara, treats the three ways as complementary. The way of action (*karma yoga*) and the way of devotion (*bhakti yoga*) are both preparations for the final way of knowledge (*jnana yoga*). Sankara insists that finally it is knowledge that brings liberation from the illusion of separation from *Brahman*. Only knowledge can dispel ignorance, and while ignorance remains liberation is impossible. Devotion to *Saguna Brahman*, or to an incarnation, such as Krishna or Rama, carries the devotee beyond attachment to the world. Devoted service purifies the mind and heart. All of which is essential preparatory work. But the last crucial step is to remove every trace of the belief that the individual is separate from *Brahman*. Whilst he believes in the need to worship God, to pray to God, to praise God, or to serve God as something existing apart from himself, he believes in duality and cannot realize unity. The self as ego must be utterly lost before the self as *Brahman* is found. '*Aham Brahmasmi*' ('I am *Brahman*') allows no separation of any degree.

Advaita Vedanta thus incorporates the way of devotion without any concessions to Vaisnavism or any other form of dualistic faith. Its monism is uncompromising. This marks it out as a strictly philosophical doctrine, and explains why theistic systems, such as that of Ramanuja, have had more direct influence upon religion in India. But for an *advaitin*, of course, it explains why *Advaita* Vedanta is the one holy tradition that underlies all faiths. Any form of devotion to God is a movement towards liberation, but faith alone is insufficient. Knowledge of unity is necessary, and the holy tradition of *Advaita* offers this, the crowning gem of enlightenment.

Yet teachers in this holy tradition have not, by any means, reduced the way of devotion to a mere appendage of the way of knowledge. At the final stage of self-realization they see no difference between love and knowledge. Hanuman, the monkey-servant of Rama in the *Ramayana*, describes himself as the slave of his master on the level of the body, his friend on the level of mind, but as one with Rama on the level of truth. In contrast to Ramanuja's view that all knowledge requires an object, so that *Brahman* itself is an object to the perception of the purified souls, *Advaita* asserts that in love there is no concept whatsoever of subject and object. Love seems to become co-extensive with the consciousness of *Brahman*, which is not conscious of anything at all, since nothing else exists.

Similarly love has been presented in *Advaita* as a kind of universal 'in-between', or medium, uniting otherwise separate creatures. If anything other than love stands between, then what arises instead is greed, anger, envy or other such obstacles to union. Attachment sums up the various forms that these intermediaries take. Without attachment love alone intervenes, making for unity. A story like that of Shakespeare's *Othello* demonstrates this. The ideas sown by Iago grow in Othello's mind to turn love into jealousy, and finally into murderous hatred. Attachment has dispossessed love, or rather love has been seemingly transmuted into forms of attachment.

Ramana Maharshi also does not belittle devotion as a means to realization. He describes the devotee as first praying for absorption in *Brahman*, then surrendering himself by faith and concentration. 'In place of the original "I", perfect self-surrender leaves a residuum of God in which "I" is lost.' Such a devotee must be moved by an eagerness equal to that of a man held forcibly under water and struggling to rise to the surface to avoid drowning. Maharshi, too, deals with the apparent duality of love by emphasizing its singularity. Love of an object must be distinguished from love in itself, for 'the self is love, in other words, God is love.' And he is fiercely critical of those who qualify *Advaita*:

> 'They persist in affirming that the individuals are part of the Supreme – his limbs as it were. Their traditional doctrine says also that the individual soul should be made

pure and then surrendered to the Supreme; then the ego
is lost and one goes to the regions of Vishnu after one's
death; then finally there is the enjoyment of the Supreme!
To say that one is apart from the Primal Source is itself a
pretension; to add that one divested of the ego becomes
pure and yet retains individuality only to enjoy or serve
the Supreme, is a deceitful stratagem. What duplicity is this
– first to appropriate what is really His, and then pretend
to experience or serve Him!'

(*Talks*, p. 183)

In the final analysis, *Advaita* Vedantists cannot accommodate the
philosophy of Ramanuja. They may interpret the way of devotion
to bring it into conformity with the principle of the real identity
of *jiva* and *Brahman*, but they cannot qualify the oneness of
Brahman. Its unity allows not a shadow of difference or other-
ness. If Vaisnavism, or any other theist standpoint, puts forward
the idea of a soul eternally distinct from *Brahman*, then it is
confusing the ego with the truly eternal principle in Man, which
is nothing less than *Brahman* itself, one and indivisible. Ramanuja
claimed to show that loss of the ego does not involve loss of individuality. But what are his freed individual souls, devoid of all
distinctive qualities as men, animals or plants; atomic, totally
dependent upon *Brahman*, and yet somehow existing eternally
as separate conscious beings? To an *advaitin* this is indeed a bleak
prospect of freedom, a kind of limbo of eternal separation from
the very love to which, when not free, the soul had aspired.

Madhva and dualism

The progression from the pure *Advaita* of Sankara to the qualified *Advaita*, or theism, of Ramanuja was bound to lead to outright
dualism in some form. Madhva, a 13th-century teacher from south
India, put forward an overtly dualistic form of Vedanta, and
attracted wide support amongst Hindus. Wherever it was regarded
as the central aspect of Vedanta, *bhakti*, with its root concept of

worship of a god by a devotee, was certain to demand an under-pinning in dualism.

Christianity in India, associated with the belief that St Thomas established churches on the Malabar coast of the southwest, seems to have had some influence on the teaching of Madhva. He was believed by his followers to be an incarnation of Vayu, the god of air or spirit. Vayu was seen as the son and agent of Vishnu. Legends grew up of Madhva's miracles, which resemble those of Christ: feeding the multitudes with a modicum of food, walking on water, stilling the raging sea, and others.

More prosaically, Madhva wrote commentaries on the major scriptures, in which he interpreted them in terms of the dualism of God and the world. Like Ramanuja, he rejected the concept of *maya* and the whole idea of the world as illusion. Unlike Ramanuja, he did not believe that the world is the body of God. Hence nature, not God, is the material cause of the world. God, souls and matter exist eternally in real separation, and individual souls and particles of matter are all permanently separated in reality as atomic units. Souls of gods, men, animals and plants have features unique to each individual, even when freed eternally from material bodies, unlike the identical souls of Ramanuja's system. Moreover, souls do not all have the same opportunity of becoming free. Some are condemned by their misdeeds to eternal damnation, some to perpetual cycles of embodiment, and some, for their virtues, to become free and contemplate, forever in bliss, the majesty of God. For this latter result, however, they need the grace of God. Thus Madhva accepted the concept of *karma*, but gave it a Calvinist sense of predestination, which raised questions of free will and divine intervention.

Three fundamental issues underlie Madhva's dualism, and distinguish it from *Advaita* Vedanta: the non-identity of *Brahman* and the individual self, or *jiva*; the nature of bondage and liber-ation; and the status of ignorance. Madhva's radical dualism led him to attack Sankara's monism from the outset. At the beginning of his commentary on the *Brahma Sutra*, Madhva argues against the idea that any valid investigation of *Brahman* could even begin from the standpoint of unity.

> 'If the subject of the inquiry viz. *Brahman*, were to be identical with the self (of the inquirer himself), the inquiry could not be pursued meaningfully; for one's own self has necessarily to be admitted as a self-evident and self-shining principle of consciousness (*svaprakasa*). Such a principle cannot be made an object of inquiry without forfeiting its self-luminosity. The proposed inquiry can thus be made meaningful only on the basis of a clear admission of the fact that *Brahman* which is the subject matter of this *Sastra* (treatise) and of this proposed inquiry is not and cannot be the same as the individual soul (*Pratyagatman*) but must be entirely different and distinct from it.'
>
> *(The Brahma Sutras and their Principal Commentaries,*
> Vol. I, p. 55)

Advaita's response to this is that, since only *Brahman* is real, the investigation by the aspirant is itself part of the illusion which that very investigation will reveal. From the start, Madhva treats the aspirant as a real separate being; hence his argument is, in fact, circular. Of course, the *advaitin* also takes a stand on the illusory nature of the separate aspirant, so this issue alone cannot resolve the matter.

On the question of bondage and liberation, there is the same crux with regard to reality. Sankara views both as illusory, as the story of the donkeys, who thought themselves bound, illustrates. Madhva regards bondage as real. The individual arrogates to himself 'independence of initiative in its dealings with its God-given environments and treats the gifts of body, senses, intellect etc. as its own independent personal possessions. It thus becomes a slave to their attractions. This is known as bondage.' (*The Brahmasutras and their Principal Commentaries*, Vol. 1, p. 56.) Such a view resembles that of *Advaita*, except for the crucial point that the self that does this is regarded by Madhva as a real, separate being.

It follows from this that the third issue, ignorance, also concerns the concept of reality. For Sankara the one fundamental, though illusory, mistake is to believe that the world is real. For Madhva, the real soul makes mistakes, but these are mistakes within a real material world. They lead the individual into a career of upward or downward movement in *karma*. It is the real ignorance of individuals that makes intervention by divine grace an essential aspect of Madhva's thought. Knowledge cannot bring release, because it only removes ignorance and not the real effects of ignorance.

Dualism obviates the difficulties associated with the *Advaita* concepts of *maya* and ignorance. There is no doubt that the *advaitin* finds it hard to explain the nature of *maya* and the origin of ignorance. Yet he would reply that these difficulties are simply inherent in the human situation. In so far as the individual believes himself to be separate, he believes in *maya*, the world of illusion. How can he, as an individual, understand the nature of that illusion, if he does not fully realize that what he calls himself – the ego – is part of it? After realization there is no illusion, so he can no longer have any questions to ask about it. Similarly, ignorance is in the possession of the illusory individual. He does not really possess it, so how can he be expected to explain its cause? Madhva, on the other hand, denies that *maya* makes any sense, and regards ignorance as possessed by the soul. Yet he suffers from the much greater difficulty of explaining how dualism is consistent with the scriptures that he reveres, particularly the Upanishads. It appears to put great strain on statements such as 'I am *Brahman*' and 'The self is *Brahman*' to deny the identity of the individual self and the universal self. In addition, there are the problems that follow from trying to explain what is the relationship between two, and indeed an infinity of, real entities – God, souls and particles of matter. On grounds of simplicity alone, *Advaita* would always win any debate with both theism and dualism.

Chapter 10

Language

Name and form

Language occupies a central place in the philosophy of Vedanta. In this respect there is a curious parallel with 20th-century philosophy in the Western world. In both cases philosophers have concluded that language is not simply a means or vehicle to express philosophical ideas, in the same way in which it expresses scientific, historical and other forms of thought, but rather that language itself is intimately bound up with questions about knowledge, mind, personal identity and so on. Both Vedantists and British 'linguistic philosophers', for example, would agree that to speak correctly is to avoid philosophical error, and that incorrect language may involve blunders that are philosophical, rather than merely grammatical. Oddly enough, their reasons for this view are perhaps diametrically opposed. The modern philosopher, following Wittgenstein, might claim that there is nothing wrong with ordinary language, but philosophical language creates errors of its own; whereas the Vedantist would argue that ordinary language misleads and requires analysis to remove false philosophical assumptions.

A simple example indicates the difference. Wittgenstein regarded an assertion such as 'I see a jar' as quite accurate, whether it happens to be true or false, and attempts to analyze it into statements about sense-data, or into conditional or 'as if' statements, as creating unnecessary problems. Vedantists, on the contrary, regard such an assertion as misleading on the grounds that it attributes an independent existence both to an individual perceiver and to an object called a jar. In each case language is examined for philosophical error, but which language contains the errors is very much at issue.

A sentence quoted earlier from the *Chandogya* Upanishad (*see* p. 31) encapsulates the Vedantic standpoint. 'All transformation has speech as its basis, and it is name only.' Transformation refers to the apparent modification of the one substance of consciousness into a multitude of forms. The world appears as a mass of individual entities – physical objects, living organisms, animals, people, processes, actions, events – whereas in reality they are all *Brahman*. Each of these entities is discriminated in language by a word or name. But these words are not merely labels, placed, as it were, upon pre-existing things. Language creates the things. *Brahman* seems to undergo transformation into a multitude, because the agency of words creates the illusion of multiplicity. A jar is nothing but consciousness under limitations imposed by the word 'jar'. As the ancient grammarian, Bhartrhari, puts it: 'jar' points to *Brahman* through the form of a jar as though one sees the world through a tube.

Sankara, who followed his predecessor Bhartrhari in many respects, used the expression 'name and form' on two levels. As a compound word in the singular (in Sanskrit), he meant by it the fundamental word '*OM*', understood as the efficient cause of all words and therefore of all transformations of *Brahman* or consciousness. He used 'names and forms' as a plural term, on the other hand, to refer to the level of the created world, in which things are themselves no more than names and forms perceived through the senses. As always, Sankara draws upon the authority of the Upanishads:

> 'There are no chariots, nor animals to be yoked to them, nor roads here, but he creates the chariots, animals and roads.'
>
> (*Brihadaranyaka*, IV iii 10)

The creation of dream objects seems to be entirely the work of the dreamer's mind, employing concepts or words to turn consciousness into many forms. Just so, concludes Sankara, are the objects of the waking state – the world – the work of words transforming consciousness into apparently real chariots, animals and roads. In this case, however, creation is clearly not by an individual, but 'is really an act of God', for the individual cannot create mountains, rivers and so on.

This latter point is of great importance, for it demonstrates that Sankara, and Vedanta in general, in no way interprets the doctrine of name and form subjectively, in the sense that objects in the world are mere impressions in the minds of individuals. The statement quoted before from the *Brahma Sutra Bhasya* (*see* pp. 29–30) makes this explicit.

> 'Not that anybody cognises a perception to be a pillar, a wall etc.; rather all people cognise a pillar, a wall, etc., as objects of perception.'
>
> (*Brahma Sutra Bhasya*, p. 419)

How then can we understand the idea that wordly objects are mere names and forms, if the individual who perceives them does not himself attribute name and form to them?

One approach is to ask what an individual actually perceives on looking at a jar. He cannot see more than a single aspect of the jar at any one time. Even over time he can see only a few of the infinite aspects that the jar may present. In a sense, he never sees the whole jar. Yet he says, with some justification, 'I see a jar'. The word 'jar', as it were, completes his picture of the jar. It somehow embodies all the other essential aspects of the jar, including non-visual ones, such as its ability to ring when struck, or shatter when dropped. Bhartrhari adds the reservation that the features peculiar to that particular jar are not included in the meaning of 'jar', only the universals that constitute its 'jar-ness'. What then is the jar, if not something created by the word? But, replies the empirical idealist, the person who sees the jar also speaks the word. Therefore, he, the perceiver, creates the jar, albeit by language. Not so, says the Vedantist. Language is not an individual matter. Words are not made up by individuals, nor even by collections of individuals in society. They come from the fundamental word '*OM*'.

Such an argument has concluded with what Vedanta, in fact, regards as the starting point. All language is derived from *OM*, the name of *Brahman* itself. '*OM*' in Sanskrit consists of three sounds or letters – 'A', 'U', and 'M', pronounced as 'u' in 'sun', 'oo' in 'soot' and 'm' in 'sum'. The 'A' and 'U' merge to become the 'O' (as in 'go') of '*OM*'. In Vedanta, 'A' represents in a variety of contexts the sustaining god Vishnu, the *guna sattva* and the organ of *chitta*, but it is essentially the sound that runs through all language. 'U' is the creative aspect of language, hence its association with the creator god Brahma, *rajas* – the *guna* of movement – , and the creative organ of mind, *buddhi*. 'M' is the letter whose sound brings things to rest; Mahesha, or Siva, *tamas* and *ahankara* (ego) are represented by it.

All sound, and hence all language, is said to be derived from *OM*. Since *OM* is the name of *Brahman*, this view of the omnipresence of *OM* parallels the idea that *Brahman* is the material and efficient cause of the universe. From the standpoint of language, *OM* is the efficient cause of everything, and some grammarians, notably Bhartrhari, regard *OM* as the material cause also, on the grounds that word and consciousness are an 'intertwined unity'.

Words and sentences

Bhartrhari, who lived in the 7th century AD, wrote a great deal about words, sentences and meaning in his exposition of grammar, the *Vakyapradiya*. He raised such difficult problems as how a word can convey anything, since each letter is heard consecutively. Since no single letter carries the meaning, then a succession of separate letters can hardly do so. He also denied that the memory of each letter consecutively was sufficient to establish a meaning for the whole word, on the grounds that each memory is also a discrete experience having no connection with other letters or memories of them. Bhartrhari's solution was to claim that the meaning emerges gradually, letter by letter, and that the final letter enables meaning to be conveyed by a kind of explosion of consciousness, called a *sphota*. Thus he distinguished between the sound of each letter, the word and the meaning.

Yet Bhartrhari realized that the same argument applies to the words in a sentence. Consequently he put forward the idea of a sentence-*sphota*, emerging on the completion of each sentence and carrying the whole meaning of the sentence. Since the sentence meaning cannot be obtained merely from the consecutive addition of each word meaning, it follows that words only have meaning by a kind of abstraction from the primary vehicle of the sentence. This implies, amongst other things, that in two similar sentences, such as 'The black dog runs' and 'The white dog runs', there is no common sentence, viz: 'The dog runs', to which the meaningful words 'black' and 'white' are added. Each of the two complete sentences carries its own meaning as an indivisible unit. 'White' and 'black' take their meaning from the sentence which contains them.

Sankara accepted much of what Bhartrhari wrote, with the important exception of the concept of *sphota*. By an Occam's razor argument Sankara claimed that meaning is indeed borne by a sentence unit, and that word meanings are mere abstractions, but that positing *sphotas* for words and sentences unnecessarily multiplies the concepts concerned. The separate parts (letters or words) form a whole (word or sentence respectively), just as trees form a forest without the simultaneous perception of every tree. Since language is the expansion of the fundamental word *OM*, it possesses the power of *Brahman* itself to form a unity which is greater than the sum of the constituent parts.

An interesting parallel with the views of Wittgenstein can be drawn here. He also set much store by the use of words. A word, he wrote, is like a piece in chess. Its meaning is the use it has in a particular language game. In itself the word, like a chess piece, is a meaningless object. Understood in relation to its role in the appropriate game – such as describing, commanding, questioning or pretending – the word, or chess piece, has a function. It comes alive, as it were. Thus Wittgenstein also sees words as drawing meaning necessarily from being embedded in sentences. He takes as an example the sentence 'Bring me a slab!' spoken by a man on a building site. He might equally well say just 'Slab!' in the context where the man he addresses knows that this means the former sentence. But then the single word takes its meaning from a whole sentence, of which it is an abbreviation. Why, on the contrary, should the sentence not be a circumlocution of the meaningful single word 'Slab!' asks Wittgenstein. He answers that the word alone would be ambiguous. It could mean, for example, 'Take the slab away!' Hence its actual meaning depends on the possibility of there being a range of relevant sentences, each of which give it a particular meaning. It could not stand alone in the language, any more than a chess piece can stand alone (*See Philosophical Investigations*, S17–20).

Attempts to give single words independent meanings break down in other respects. If one utters the word 'tree', says Bhartrhari, it only conveys meaning if the grammatical predicate 'exists' is implied. By a similar argument, Western logicians have introduced an existential quantifier into the analysis of sentences in which the existence of the subject is implied but not asserted. 'The king of Albania is called Zog' implies that there is a king of Albania. Moreover, Bhartrhari explains that the use of grammatical terms to inflect individual words, as in noun case endings and the conjugation of verbs, also goes to prove that words cannot stand alone. Modern languages, such as English, that are not heavily inflected, can be said to imply inflection by such means as word position in the sentence. Certainly, without the identification of the syntactical role of a word, language would become impossible.

Grammar

This brings us to another key feature of language, which Vedanta interprets as having profound philosophical significance, namely the grammatical structure of sentences. Here we must turn to the greatest of all grammarians, the 4th-century BC formulator of the rules of classical Sanskrit, Panini. In his *Astadhyayi* (Eight Chapters), he explained, amongst much else, how the other words in a sentence are related grammatically to the verb. This emphasis on the verb implies that sentences essentially denote actions (which includes the 'action' of existing), and is in keeping with the Vedantic standpoint that the world is made of processes, rather than of ontologically independent things. Plato similarly believed that the world is in a state of becoming rather than of being.

Interestingly, Panini begins with what Western grammarians call the ablative case, which in English is conveyed usually by the use of the preposition 'from'. This is used, he writes, for whatever stands as the unmoving point from which the movement denoted by the verb originates. He gives as one example the action of learning from a teacher. The word 'teacher' is in the ablative case, because the teacher is, or contains, the unmoving point or origin of the act of teaching. Since the Sanskrit word used for the unmoving point also carries the meaning of 'eternal', there is a philosophical implication that the ultimate source of all action is *Brahman*.

Panini's second case is the dative, denoted in English by 'to', or simply by an indirect object. Here he concludes that whatever or whoever the agent intends to connect with the action takes this case when it consists of some kind of giving or sacrificing. For example, this includes the promisee of the act of promising and the creditor of owing, but more generally it relates to the dedication of the agent. The free will of the agent arises from his ability to dedicate any action to something of his own choosing, whether *Brahman*, a god, or his own pleasure, so that the dative case also covers more than may be explicit in a normal transitive sentence. An intransitive verb, such as 'walk', may actually bear the sense of the walking being dedicated to *Brahman*, even when there is no grammatical indirect object in the sentence.

Thirdly, Panini describes the instrumental case – usually

covered by the ablative in Western grammar and in English by 'with' or 'by' – as that which is most propitious for the accomplishing of the action, such as an axe for cutting wood. His aphorism (sutra) on this case uses the superlative, suggesting that in any action the instrument in fact to hand is the most suitable – for example, there is an implication that an axe is the best instrument for cutting wood. Such a brief grammatical point contains a whole philosophical approach to action, ranging from 'the bad workman always blames his tools' to the acceptance of oneself as a fit instrument of God.

Next comes what may be called the locative, relating to the place, and also to the time, of the action – the where and when. Panini refers to this as the support or substratum, rather than merely the spatio-temporal position. Thus 'He sits in the chair', with 'chair' in the locative case, carries the sense of the subject being supported, not merely by a physical chair, but more fundamentally by a substance of which the chair is just a manifestation. Once more the grammar indicates a profound ontology rather than mere existence in the physical world. Space and time are locations of physical events, time alone perhaps of mental ones, but all action can be understood as occurring within the universal substance of *Brahman*, or consciousness. Hence the word in the locative case in a sentence may draw the speaker or hearer back to reality itself.

The object, in the case of transitive verbs, is said by Panini to be that which is most desired by the subject of the verb. Obviously verbs like 'to hate' or 'to strike' appear to conflict with this, but Panini includes examples such as 'He eats the poison' and 'He sees the thieves'. The concept of intention is relevant here, since the poison may be eaten intentionally without knowing that it is poison, or eaten with the intention of killing oneself. Similarly, the victim of thieves may desire to see them, if not to be robbed by them. In each case the subject does what he most desires. Desire in Vedanta is understood as the prime mover of action, rather than as a feeling of wanting something. In this sense all actions involving transitive verbs are motivated by desire for the intended object of the action.

Finally, the sixth case is the subject of the verb. Panini describes this with the aphorism: 'The subject has the system within himself.' System means here the manifestation of law. Thus the subject contains the law that governs the action. As the originator of the action, the subject may also be called its cause. This needs to be seen in the context of the Vedantic principle that the self does not act. The subject as such is not the self but rather the ego, acting under desire yet embodying the law that determines the nature and effect of the action. Such a meaning carries the sense of the speaker observing his own action and watching himself as an agent, rather than of 'doing' as a subject. Reference to oneself in the third person – as used, for example, by Julius Caesar and Charles de Gaulle – has a flavour of this.

Sanskrit contains two other grammatical cases not directly related to a verb. The vocative, used for addressing someone or something (O table!), is described by Panini with a word the root of which means 'to wake up'! The genitive case primarily covers relations between nouns, especially possession, not involving a verb – for instance, 'the king's man', 'the beast's foot' – though in practice it is sometimes used in Sanskrit variously for the instrumental, dative, locative or accusative (object) cases – as also in English occasionally.

It is clear from Panini's exposition that he is not merely giving an analysis of case endings as they happen to be used in Sanskrit. As a Vedantist, he does not view language as a system of labels placed by convention upon the processes of the 'real' world. His sutras refer as much to the processes themselves as to the words and sentences. In other words, he is analyzing both word and action, for they are the same in so far as 'all transformation is name only.' Every action actually has a still point from which it emerges, a dedication, an instrument best suited to it, a substratum beyond place and time, a subject who expresses the law that governs it, and – sometimes – an object desired. Hence the study of grammar is, at the same time, a study of nature (*prakriti*), and the laws of grammar are the laws of nature.

This comprehensive view of grammar is alien to modern Western thought, which by regarding it as a set of purely conventional rules has relegated it to insignificance. The philosophical approach of Vedanta to grammar, however, is by no means limited to Panini's striking analysis of action. Panini himself covers every aspect of Sanskrit grammar in about 4,000 *sutras.*

One other area that he deals with at length may be mentioned to illustrate the principle of the *Chandogya* Upanishad. As with all languages, Sanskrit, when spoken, contains changes of sound incurred by the junction of letters. These may occur within words or between them, and at the junction of vowels, consonants or one of each. For example, in English 's' followed by 'h' becomes the new sound 'sh'. Panini, with enormous patience, states these rules – called *sandhi* – explicitly. They appear to be rules of language, but Panini clearly regards them as laws of nature, in the sense of natural laws of sound. But they can also be understood as the laws that govern the meeting of actual things or persons in the 'real' world. When physical surfaces touch, a new event occurs, like a grating, crashing, sliding or bruising. When people meet their lives may be changed. When certain historical events are sequential, history may change course. Laws of *sandhi* are undoubtedly present in the world. Moreover, if, as Vedanta claims, everything arises from the fundamental sound of *OM*, the sound of an event is certainly instrumental to its outcome.

Levels of speech

Following a reference in the Rig Veda to four levels of speech, Bhartrhari developed this idea and related it to the creation of a sentence. At the deepest level of the speaker, language has no formulation of any kind and no differentiation. It exists simply as the pure knowledge, or the Veda, present in the individual. It is a desire that activates the power of speech. When the individual has the desire to say something, an impulse of sound passes into a kind of matrix, called *pashyanti* (literally 'seeing'). Bhartrhari describes this second level as like the yoke of an egg, where differentiation of sounds and an inner sequence is held in potential, or 'merged' as he puts it. The forms of objects of knowledge are said to have entered at this stage. It is followed by a movement into the third level, called *madhyama* (intermediate state). Here the sound 'looks as if it has sequence'. This is the first point of formulation, where differentiation emerges, and sounds become identifiable and related to meaning. It is recognizable by the individual as the condition of having something to say, but not having yet explicitly formulated the words and sentence to say it. Finally, the full formulation occurs with the participation of the vocal organs in the mouth and the emergence of audible sound. This last level is called *vaikhari* (elaborated speech).

Bhartrhari's account of these four levels raises many questions. Firstly, how is all this related to the individual human organism? One answer to this is to refer each level of speech to a definite physical location. *Vaikhari* is obviously associated with the mouth, and in particular with the tongue. *Madhyama* may be located in the larynx; *pashyanti* in the heart; and the deepest level, which is called *para* (furthest or ultimate), in the navel. Such physical ascriptions can be taken, perhaps, as associations rather than literal locations.

Secondly, there is the question of what language is being referred to. The level of audible speech clearly uses the speaker's own native or acquired language – English, Hindi or whatever. *Madhyama* would appear to be the process of assembling the elements of this language, with the intention of expressing the idea derived from *pashyanti*; hence the feeling of having something in memory or 'on the tip of one's tongue', without actually being in a position to say it audibly. What language then does *pashyanti* utilize? This raises the significant question of whether there is a natural language, in some sense prior to spoken languages, which embodies the idea created in the mind of the speaker.

Consider the word 'mother'. Without this word, the relationship of mother and child would not exist. There would simply be two human beings, whose only relationship would occur in the process of physical birth. All the qualities associated with motherhood – care, love, protection and so on – are dependent on the word 'mother'. Yet no one word in any particular language is essential for this relationship to exist. Moreover, animals exhibit the characteristics of motherhood without appearing to have language at all. Therefore the word 'mother' may be thought to have a more universal paradigm, a kind of Platonic form, in a natural language. If so, this language is the content of the level of *pashyanti*.

Little can be said of the language at the ultimate level of *para*. Its whole content is the word *OM*, the name of *Brahman*, analogous to the Word of St John's gospel from which all things are created. According to the doctrine of *Shabda Brahman* (Word *Brahman*), expounded by Bhartrhari, everything is created by sound, and hence from this fundamental word.

This naturally leads to a third and most challenging problem of the Vedantic view of language. How can the levels of speech identified in the individual be reconciled with the universal nature of language as the source and efficient cause of the world itself? A similar question has already been encountered in relation to the description in the *Mandukya* Upanishad of the states of waking, dream and sleep and the underlying unity of consciousness (*see* pp. 71–9). How can one individual's waking state be understood as the very same thing as the whole objective world? Likewise, how does an individual person speak the world into existence? As Sankara says, no person makes the mountains or rivers – nor indeed even a jar – by means of speech.

Once more the argument turns on the most fundamental question of all – that of how *Advaita* is possible. If each person is an independent self, opposed to the world, including other people, which each individual observes as external to himself, then there is an irreconcilable gap between the individual self who speaks and the one universal language which creates the objects of the world. The two doctrines of levels of speech, on one hand, and the creative omnipotence of *OM*, on the other, cannot both be true. If, however, the doctrine of the individual's ability to bring speech from the profundity of pure knowledge to the audible vernacular is understood in a universal sense, the problem can at least be viewed coherently, if not truly comprehended.

The *Mandukya* Upanishad offers us the key. The waking state is at once a state of *buddhi* and a description of the external world. If the ego is abandoned altogether, then *buddhi* itself is universal, not a merely personal state of a separate mind. So, too, may *vaikhari* be a state of audible speech and, at the same time, the names and forms that constitute the things of the physical world of which our senses inform us. An utterance of the word 'chair' does not simply create a chair out of thin air, but perceiving something as a chair is dependent upon the ability to use the word. The individual's personal perception of the chair is not at issue here. It is only an aspect of the chair that is perceived and not the chair itself. Only the word is the whole chair. Bhartrhari himself rejected any possibility of direct perception, devoid of words, between an observer and an object.

Similarly, the level of *madhyama* corresponds to the dream state. The inner world, presented in time but not in space, is mental. Everything it contains – chariots, animals, roads and the rest – is created by words without any formulation as audible speech. Differentiation of the original idea is sufficient to give rise to mental objects. Dream objects are like embryonic 'real' objects; they are almost there but not quite. Memory has drawn them from their 'yoke' condition in *pashyanti*. But this dream state, though it may seem to be the individual mind of one person, is in reality the cosmic mind in which words and sentences are formed as universals.

In the *Mandukya*, deep sleep is described as a condition where 'everything becomes undifferentiated', and which is 'the doorway to the experience of the dream and waking states'. Here there is no sequence, only the potential for sequence; no objects, only the potential for objects. On a universal level this deep sleep is the unmanifested nature of the world. The *Mandukya* further calls it 'omniscient, the inner director of all, the place of origin and dissolution of all beings.' The forms of objects of knowledge have entered, but are not separately discernible. On the side of language, the one word *OM* has begun to express itself as the names and forms of everything.

Likewise the *Mandukya*'s description of *Brahman* as the unchanging, non-dual self in which all phenomena cease, corresponds to the state of *para*, where knowledge itself is held, totally undifferentiated and unified in the one fundamental sound *OM*. There is no conceivable place here for the individual. It is evident then that the doctrine of Word *Brahman* is intrinsically reliant upon the central principle of *Advaita* Vedanta. No dualistic philosophy could sustain a theory of language which contained both an account of how language emerges through four levels apparently identifiable within one person and an account of the creation of the world as name and form only. If all transformation is by name only, then name cannot be the possession of an individual. Names and forms, as Sankara says, are no more than the apparent development of the one name-form. Such a development may appear to the ignorant individual as occurring in himself, but in reality it occurs in the one self of which he, as an individual, is the merest shadow.

Sanskrit

No account of Vedanta would be complete without some reference to the Sanskrit language, if only because all the great literature of Vedanta is written in Sanskrit – the four Vedas, the Upanishads, the *Bhagavad Gita*, the *Brahma Sutra Bhasya*, the *Ramayana*, the *Mahabharata*, the *Astadhaya*, the *Vakyapradiya* and much else. For millennia Sanskrit has been passed on from generation to generation of scholars by oral learning and teaching, with virtually no change in the language of the works that are regarded as *sruti* (revealed knowledge) and *smriti* (remembered knowledge). The attitude of such devoted scholars is summed up by the sage who proclaimed that the accurate pronunciation of a short 'A' sound is of more importance than the birth of a son!

Western scholars, such as Sir William Jones in the 18th century and Max Müller and Monier Monier-Williams in the 19th century, recognized the unique place that Sanskrit holds. Indo-European languages have largely evolved from it, so that many words and grammatical constructions can be traced back to Sanskrit. In particular, its system of *dhatus*, or roots, is the source of central areas of Indo-European vocabularies. '*As*', to be; '*jna*', to know; '*gam*', to go; '*stha*', to stand; '*raj*', to reign are a few examples. What has impressed Western scholars most, however, is probably the comprehensive nature of Sanskrit grammar, as revealed by Panini and generations of grammarians. Every word in a Sanskrit sentence has a precise grammatical function, usually shown by inflection. Tense, voice, number, gender, case and *sandhi* are all explicit to a greater extent than in any other recorded language. At the same time this extraordinary precision is combined with great flexibility to take account of the meaning of a sentence on any particular occasion of its utterance. Sanskrit words, for example, have a very wide range of meanings, determined by place, time, association, context, related words and so on. For speech is paramount in the use of Sanskrit, as the philosophy of Word *Brahman* makes clear. What matters especially is the sound of the language. Its written form has always been subordinate, albeit vital in the preservation of accurate spelling and grammar.

Word *Brahman* as a major strand in Vedantic teaching offers a philosophical discipline by means of the study of Sanskrit. The student begins at the level of *vaikhari*, and by diligent practice seeks to penetrate the next two levels to reach the knowledge in *para*. He begins with the purification of the pronunciation of letters, words and sentences. Vowel sounds, of which there are nine, are particularly important because they are said to be the source of the sixteen *shakti*, or powers, of *Brahman*, which give emotional force to actions. Attention is given to audibility, sweet-

ness and the three measures of short, long and prolonged vowel
sounds. (There are seven extra forms of the vowels). Clear understanding of meaning and grammar follows, including the construction of words from *dhatus* by modification of vowels and the
addition of prefixes and suffixes. Here the sentence is given due
prominence as the basic unit of speech, for – as Bhartrhari emphasized – the multiplicity of things cognized does not affect the unity
of the cognition.

This leads back to the ideas lodged in *madhyama*, the mental
level. Philosophical principles are introduced at this stage to
eliminate false ideas, especially of duality. As Bhartrhari said, 'The
attainment of *Brahman* is nothing more than going beyond the
knot of the ego-sense in the form of "I" and "mine"'. Finally comes
the purification of *pashyanti* with the use of meditation or other
practices aimed at stillness. The fourth level of *para* is untouched
by movement or ignorance of any kind, and requires no teaching
or technique. Once more Vedanta follows the principle that in
truth everything is already perfect, so that all effort is directed to
the removal of obstacles. Thus the study of the Sanskrit language
may become a means to the realization of *Brahman.*

Chapter 11

Law and Society

Dharma

The Sanskrit word *dharma* can be translated simply as 'law', but it has a wider significance than the English word. Indeed its dictionary meanings include morality, justice, practice, virtue, conduct and religion. By derivation it means that which is established or firm; hence it carries the sense of holding or preserving. Laws of nature, like those of gravity or thermodynamics, clearly hold physical things to definite forms of movement or change. Without such laws events would occur randomly or chaotically. Similarly, the laws of a nation hold people to certain courses of action. They may transgress the law, but then the outcome is determined by rule or law.

This simple point about the holding quality of law in respect to both physical things and to human society helps to elucidate the comprehensive nature of *dharma*. Western thought makes a fairly clear distinction between prescriptive and descriptive law. As recently as the 18th century this distinction was not always made. The great legal writer, William Blackstone, defined law as a 'rule of action prescribed by some superior, and which the inferior is bound to obey.' Thus, for Blackstone, physical events conformed to laws laid down by God, just as men conformed to laws laid down by a sovereign. No doubt the decline in religious belief since

Blackstone's time has contributed to the idea that physical laws are not established by a creator as law-giver and that human laws are merely prescribed by governments. Since Vedanta is centred upon the concept of *Brahman* as a supreme, indeed infinite, power, which is the source of all law, there is no significant bifurcation between prescriptive and descriptive law in its system. *Dharma* is the law of *Brahman* throughout the creation. The law for men and the law for things are at root one law.

One way of explaining the unity of law in Vedanta is to see it as inherent in nature (*prakriti*). Everything has a nature, both material things and living organisms – in particular, human beings. The nature of anything constitutes the law for that thing. It contains, as it were, the law in its essence. It is the law that a particular chemical substance will react in a set way in certain conditions. So too it is the law that a mustard seed grows into a mustard plant, that a lion roars and that men and women walk on two feet and speak with their vocal chords. There is an obvious objection to this assimilation of humans to material things and other organisms. The chemical substance, the mustard seed and probably the lion have no choice in the matter. Man does have choice. He can crawl on all fours and refuse to speak. Therefore, one may argue, laws for men are only prescriptive, except in so far as some physical laws – and perhaps some psychological and social laws – are binding, such as those that govern the human physiological system.

Yet consider what happens if someone chooses to act differently from the 'laws' to walk or to speak. He or she comes under other 'laws', which have definite consequences. The legs and vocal chords become weak and ineffective if not used. The impact on the life of the 'refusenik' is devastating. Vedanta explains this by referring to levels of law. For law operates through the various levels of elements and *gunas*. Laws are finer at the level of intelligence than at the level of physical elements. If a man chooses to live as a brute beast, he comes under the appropriate laws. Nevertheless, argues the opponent, his very power to choose shows an important degree of independence of the law. But does it? Choice is a function of intelligence (*buddhi*), which is itself governed by law. Intelligence under *sattva* leads to one choice; under *rajas* or *tamas* to another. It is only the self in Man, as the consciousness observing his actions, which is above the *guna*, and hence above the law.

Such a standpoint seems to preclude free will (*see* pp. 108–10). But in the present moment the attitude adopted by the individual towards all that he faces is not determined. Even this is under law in its effects, but not controlled by law in its origin, for its source is consciousness itself. The present moment connects the embodied individual with *Brahman*. It can be likened to the uncaused will that Kant regarded as the whole dignity of Man, and, no doubt, to other formulations by Western thinkers. In so far as the connection is with the very source of law itself, it does not invalidate the proposition implicit in the concept of *dharma*, that the one fundamental law governs everything in creation.

In Vedanta this one law of *dharma*, of which all particular laws are instances, is the will of *Brahman*. Freedom for the individual lies in adherence to this law, as Arjuna discovered on the field of Kurukshetra. *Brahman*'s will is the necessity of the moment, in the sense of whatever needs to be done. Individuals may ignore it or follow it, though if it is seen clearly it cannot be ignored. When seen obscurely, 'through a glass darkly', it can be neglected, or performed half-heartedly; when seen with the eye of reason it is compelling. But compulsion by the law of *Brahman* is freedom. As Kant wrote, freedom is obedience to a law which we prescribe to ourselves – provided that the self is *Brahman* and not the ego! Such lawful action may be regarded as duty, though not like a worldly duty prescribed by one's family, or by social or professional responsibilities. It is an absolute or categorical duty.

How then is this awareness of universal law and the need to act upon it related to one's nature? The individual finds within himself *kartavya*, literally 'what is to be done'. His inmost nature contains this, like a seed. It is unique to each person, and may be understood as the reason for his embodiment. Yet it is quite distinct from *karma*, the inherited dispositions that mould each lifetime. These are the outcomes of previous lives, the accumulations of effects of earlier actions. They, too, are governed by law, the law of *karma*, but they constitute the conditions in which one acts in this particular life. They cannot be avoided, but nor are they totally compelling, for each human being is endowed with reason, the power to discriminate true from false, right from wrong. Hence his inner conviction of 'what needs to be done' can be heeded. *Karma* can be faced and transcended. In acting thus, the individual follows the will of *Brahman*, the one law. For him this particular unique way of acting is his path to freedom. *Karma* is an obstacle to be overcome, not an insuperable barrier to his development or movement towards realization. The fully realized man, of course, follows *dharma* at all times and in all places. His *karma* works itself out, and he creates no more of it.

A final point needs to be made. How is the recognition by the individual of 'what needs to be done' in the world around him related to his inner awareness of *kartavya*, the necessity within rooted in his nature? The answer is that they are identical. Freedom ignores the apparent dichotomy of 'inner' and 'outer'. The law is one. What needs to be done in the world is what needs to be done in the heart of the individual. In carrying out the duty laid down by *dharma* the individual is at one with the world. As a separate creature with desires and purposes of his own, he no longer exists.

> 'Rid of doubts and cleansed of every sin,
> Resolved upon the welfare of the world,
> The *rishis* [wise], also, masters of themselves,
> Absorbed in *Brahman*, find their freedom there;'
>
> (*Bhagavad Gita*, V, 25, p. 66)

Law and morality

A king was devoted to the truth. His kingdom was well-endowed and prosperous. One of the king's ways of helping his subjects was to hold a market at which anyone could bring produce to sell.

At the end of the market day, the king's officers bought all the unsold produce in order to prevent the ruin of anyone who had brought goods to the market. They would store the produce for later use or sale. A crafty trader thought that he would test the will of the king to keep his word. He brought to the market a cartload of rubbish and, since of course no one bought any, he demanded payment for it at the end of the day. The officers felt obliged to keep to the law, so they paid him for it, and the rubbish was dumped in the royal palace.

One night the goddess of wealth, Lakshmi, wife of the supreme god, Narayana, appeared before the king and announced that she was leaving his kingdom, as the palace was such a dirty place. Soon the gods and goddesses of art, wisdom, crafts, honour and other facets of the kingdom all followed her, so that it was reduced to poverty. At last Narayana came to the king and said that since all the deities, including his own wife, had left he too would depart. Whereupon the king replied 'You cannot go. You have no reason to leave me, for you are the truth itself and I am still holding to it. Only if I speak untruth may you leave.' Narayana acknowledged that the king was right. He remained in the kingdom. After a while Lakshmi returned, saying that she could not live without her husband. All the other deities eventually followed her, and the kingdom was restored to its former glory.

The king had followed *dharma*, recognizing it in himself as the constant need to speak the truth and to keep his word. The story illustrates why *dharma* is both the fundamental natural law inherent in everything and, at the same time, the law of righteousness. The king acted morally by doing what he knew to be right. At the same time the course of events in his kingdom followed the natural law inherent in the situation. Thus law and morality are both included in *dharma*. Its cardinal precepts, for example, are often stated to be non-violence, truthfulness, non-stealing, purity and restraint of senses. Modern Western concepts of law as a kind of outer constraint and morality as an inner rule or feeling do not apply here. The one law is the natural law in the sense of residing in the nature of things, so that individuals, societies and all creatures are subject to it. Man-made laws are distinct from this natural law, as are man-made moral codes, for they themselves are not *dharma*. They may be based upon or reflect *dharma*, and this for Vedanta would be the one sure test of their real authority and value.

Dharma as the common law

Until around the 19th century the Western world's concept of a natural law discoverable through reason was akin to that of *dharma*. Positivism, Marxism and other forms of modern philosophy have almost eliminated this way of thinking about law. An outstanding example of it remains, however, in the common law of England, albeit that even this is now seriously obscured by the current emphasis upon statute law. Common law is the law that has existed from time immemorial in the customs of the people. It is thus a kind of inherent tendency to rightness or justice, arising from the nature of people living together in a community. As such it can be found or discovered, rather than created or decided upon. In England it is said to reside 'in the breast of the judges', who discern it within themselves after reflection upon their knowledge and observation of its practice. The judges are learned in the law, but this is not mere book learning; nor is it the learning of laws created by kings or Parliaments. It is the learning of recorded cases and the judgments made therein. For in such cases the principles of law have been identified from their application to particular circumstances. In short, the common law is thought of as existing in the nature of the people. Such a concept comes close to that of *dharma*.

The *Laws of Manu*, probably written in the 1st century BC, but based upon more ancient practice, exhibit a similar and even more comprehensive system of law. They state that the major sources of law are the tradition and virtuous conduct of those who know the Veda, and the customs of holy men. The Veda itself is seen as the primary authority. Veda does not mean written sources, though now, of course, it is presented in its four written forms of Rig, Samur, Yajur and Atharva. The Veda is co-eval with mankind, for it is the universal knowledge implicit in humanity and residing in every heart. Thus Man knows the nature of every created thing, and the law for everything, including himself. Hence the wise, who have realized this inner knowledge, are the recourse of a society requiring law. Judges, as the Old Testament and the English common law indicate, are the lawgivers.

Yet this view of law does not rely upon a kind of intuition, least of all upon instinct. Reason is the faculty that discovers it. Plato called it the 'golden chord of reason', and history records a correlation between revivals of law and the rediscovery of Plato's use of reason, as for example in 12th-century Western Europe. Reason discovers the law by eliminating errors and contradictions, removing obscurities and recognizing the essence of the matter when it is presented before it. In Vedanta, reason is the highest function of *buddhi* or intelligence. To reveal *dharma*, the will of *Brahman*, is the finest service that reason performs.

Punishment

Although *dharma* is the law, adherence to which creates harmony, general well-being and prosperity, it is also, say the *Laws of Manu*, a bull whom the violator of the law should beware. For example:

> 'A witness who deposes in an assembly of honourable men anything else but what he has seen or heard, falls after death headlong into hell and loses heaven.'
>
> (*Laws*, VIII 75, p. 267)

Natural law ensures the just punishment of evildoers, but the king, or sovereign, is the agent by whom this punishment may be inflicted. He himself suffers most if he fails to act justly, for he is not above the law – a principle that the 13th-century legal scholar Henry Bracton stated clearly in medieval England ('The king is under no man, but under God and the law'). An unjust king 'sinks into hell'. Punishment is inflicted by the king according to the offence, ranging from minor infringements to serious crimes. For example:

> 'According to the usefulness of the several kinds of trees a fine must be inflicted for injuring them.'

> 'Men who commit adultery with the wives of others, the king shall cause to be marked by punishments which cause terror, and afterwards banish.'
>
> (*Laws*, VIII 285, p. 304; 352, p. 315)

So close is the relationship between law and punishment that the *Mahabharata* regards the latter as the principal means by which the world is maintained. 'That upon which all things depend is called chastisement.' (VIII, p. 261). At times one is reminded of Thomas Hobbes' view in *Leviathan* of the war of all against all that makes life nasty, brutish and short. 'If chastisement had not existed, all creatures would have ground one another.' (VIII, p. 262). A world without punishment is envisaged in which men make no distinctions between right and wrong conduct in matters like proper food and drink, sexual restraint, property and consideration for others in general. Then Vishnu himself shows mercy by embodying himself as chastisement, so that good order can be established.

The scope of this conception is demonstrated by the inclusion in it of time and death as agents of punishment, and by the idea that elements of nature are governed by a god who metes out due chastisement, such as ocean as the lord of rivers. Perhaps the nearest equivalent to this in Western thought is that of a kind of divine justice, whereby all creatures receive the just measure of their nature. Implied in it is the notion that no creature escapes the consequences of its own actions, a view developed in full in the law of *karma*, under which punishment extends into future lives and leaves no act unmeasured, despite the intervention of death. *Manu*, too, recognizes the inexorable grip of evil upon the human spirit.

> 'Unrighteousness, practised in this world, does not at once produce its fruit, like a cow; but, advancing slowly, it cuts off the roots of him who committed it.'
>
> (*Laws*, IV 172, p. 155)

Yet in punishment lies mercy, for without correction there would be nothing to halt the descent into darkness or hell.

Classes and caste

No subject in Indian thought and society arouses more controversy than that of caste. What is called the caste system in present day India is a complicated mixture of ancient ideas, indigenous customs and reactions to European colonialism. Hence the questions of how it operates and how it has evolved over many centuries are best left to historians and sociologists. A student of Vedanta, however, is entitled to turn to what the scriptures and teachers tell us about classifications of people in society, without the need either to justify or repudiate the present caste system. Nevertheless, it would be fair to say that that system bears little resemblance to the account which Vedanta gives.

The Sanskrit word used for the four social groups identified by Vedanta is *varna*, which means colour, covering, character or quality. It is not strictly used for caste at all, since another word, *jati*, has this meaning. For this reason we may translate *varna* as 'class' in the sense of a group determined by qualities and specific duties, none of which are, in fact, 'colour' in a racial sense. What then are these groups and what are their defining qualities and duties?

In the Rig Veda, the four classes are said to have sprung from the body of a primeval deity with the form of a man. From his mouth came forth *brahmans*, the highest class of the wise; from his arms came the *kshatriyas*, warriors and rulers; from his thighs the *vaisyas,* or traders and farmers; and from his feet the *sudras,* the lowest class, whose function is to serve the other three classes. The *Bhagavad Gita* more simply refers to the creation of classes directly by Krishna, while the *Brihadaranyaka* Upanishad and the *Mahabharata* both say that the *brahmans* were created first and the other three classes were created from them. What these explanations have in common is their insistence upon the natural division of all humans into these four classes. There is no room here for classes being determined by social conditions; they are rooted in human nature, though this does not imply that individuals cannot change class. Moreover, both the divine origin and the natural basis of the distribution of qualities imply that for each class the role that it plays is the law or *dharma* for that class. For an individual, obedience to the duties of his class is a requirement of *dharma,* in addition to his general duty to obey the law.

Krishna in the *Gita* is said to have created classes 'according to the distribution of *gunas* and actions'. In *brahmans sattva* predominates; in *kshatriyas sattva* is subordinate to *rajas*; in *vaisyas rajas* also is uppermost, but *tamas* is stronger than *sattva*; and in *sudras tamas* comes to the fore. Actions cannot be so neatly classified. In general, *brahmans* are devoted to study and teaching of the Veda, to worship and prayer, austerity, self-restraint and purity. *Kshatriyas* also study the Veda, but do not teach. Essentially they are the rulers and protectors of the people, including the *brahmans.* Hence they are strong, bold, warlike, judicial and efficient. They exhibit eloquence and artistry in what they do. *Vaisyas* know how to create wealth. The land is in their care, though it is ultimately controlled by *kshatriyas.* (In ancient India the king was the landholder, renting sites out; see *The Wonder that was India,* pp. 109–10.) On their tenancies the *vaishyas* rear livestock and grow crops. Trade and money also come within their purview. *Sudras,* by contrast, have no specific function beyond that of service to the three superior classes. They do not study, nor do they acquire wealth. They do not seek purity, and they alone are not initiated into their class (Initiation gives to the three other classes the epithet 'twice-born'.)

These brief descriptions give merely the defining actions of the four classes. Vedantic literature, in fact, portrays them with a much greater range of qualities and without the apparent rigidity. Much attention is given in the *Mahabharata*, for example, to the actions of ruling *kshatriyas*, for 'the truth is that the king makes the age'.

> 'A king possessed of intelligence should always avoid war for acquisition of territory. The acquisition of dominion should be made by the three well-known means of conciliation, gift and disunion . . . For hearing the complaints and answers of disputants in judicial suits, the king should always appoint persons possessed of wisdom and a knowledge of justice. The king should set honest and trustworthy men over his mines, salt, grain, ferries, and elephant corps. The king who always wields with propriety the rod of chastisement earns great merit . . . The king should be conversant with the Vedas and their branches, possessed of wisdom, engaged in penances, charitable, devoted to the performance of sacrifices.
>
> *(Mahabharata*, VIII, p. 152)

As for *sudras*, their treatment sometimes approaches the pathetic.

> 'It is said that *sudras* should certainly be maintained by the other orders. Worn-out umbrellas, turbans, beds and seats, shoes and fans should be given to the *sudra* servants. Torn clothes which are no longer fit for wear should be given away by the regenerate classes unto the *sudra*. These are the latter's lawful acquisitions.'
>
> *(Mahabharata*, VIII, p. 131)

The concept of class is interwoven with that of the *yuga* or historical age (*see* pp. 131–6). Some sources state that in the golden age there were no classes. All men and women were pure, virtuous and of the same character, in accordance with *Manu*'s description of the virtues common to all classes.

> 'Abstention from injuring creatures, veracity, abstention from unlawfully appropriating the goods of others, purity, and control of the organs, *Manu* has declared to be the summary of the law for the four castes.'
>
> (*Laws*, p. 416)

Alternatively the golden age is understood as a time when all four classes perform their natural duties to perfection, so that life is harmonious and society prospers.

In the silver age, evil forces threaten mankind, but the power of the *brahmans* and *kshatriyas* stands firmly against them. Rama, a silver age king portrayed in the epic *Ramayana*, is the epitome of the virtuous *kshatriya*. His defeat of Ravana, the demon in whom lust and greed have overborne divine austerity, demonstrates the role of the ruler obedient to the natural order. Rama's dependence on the advice of the *brahman* Vasishtha accords with the relationship between king and priest prescribed by the *Brihadaranya* Upanishad.

> 'Hence the king is above all men. The priest occupies a lower seat at the coronation. The priest confers the crown upon the king, is the root of the king's power. Therefore though the king attain supremacy at the end of his coronation he sits below the priest and acknowledges him as the root of his power. So whoever destroys the priest, destroys his root. He sins; he destroys the good.'
>
> (*The Ten Principal Upanishads*, p. 122)

Rama's power stems not only from the support of the *brahmans*, but also from his constant adherence to *dharma*. He never forgets that he is the servant of the law, as the Veda has taught him.

'Law is the power of the king; there is nothing higher than law. Even a weak man rules the strong with the help of law; law and the king are the same. Law is truth. Who speaks the truth, speaks the law; who speaks the law, speaks the truth; they are the same.'

(*The Ten Principal Upanishads*, p. 123)

In the *Mahabharata*, a bronze age epic, the *kshatriyas* exhibit the nature of heroic warriors, akin to those of Hesiod and Homer. Even here they greatly respect the authority of the *brahmans* and of the law, but their energy overrides their piety, and they often succumb to the blandishments of glory, arrogance or lesser vices, like the gambling of Yudhishthera. In the bronze age, especially, the *kshatriyas* define the nature of the time. Great issues and events hold the stage; life is a drama, a battleground of good and evil; however much people degenerate, there is no pettiness.

What distinguishes the age of iron is the very fact that the discrimination of classes lapses. As the *Vishnu Purana* observes, the authority of *brahmans* is no longer recognized, with a consequent falling away from respect for, or even awareness of, the Veda. *Kshatriyas* plunder the people, rather than protect them. Acquisition of wealth – a cardinal feature of the *vaishyas* – becomes a general desire of all and sundry. Those who possess chariots and elephants proclaim themselves kings. *Vaishyas* themselves abandon trade and agriculture and take to the lesser crafts or to servitude. *Sudras* become even religious mendicants, and the lowest class gradually prevail in every aspect of society. Yet still it is the real *kshatriyas* who make the age what it is, for their desertion of their duties enables such a state of confusion to arise.

Are classes hereditary?

Much debate has taken place about the question of whether or not classes in Vedanta are hereditary. The issue really turns on the meaning of being born into a particular class. It may mean inheriting class characteristics from parents, or merely possessing those class characteristics at birth. Vedic literature undoubtedly supports the latter interpretation. The *Chandogya* Upanishad, for example, makes it clear that class at birth is a result, not of parentage, but of actions in earlier lives.

> 'Among them those who were performers of meritorious deeds here, they will attain good births indeed in a quick manner – birth as a *Brahmin*, or birth as a *Kshatriya*, or birth as a *Vaisya*. On the other hand, those who were performers of bad deeds here, they will attain bad births indeed in a quick manner – birth as a dog, or birth as a pig, or birth as a *Candala* (outcast).'
>
> (*Chandogya* Upanishad, V 10 7, p. 373)

Thus class is intimately related to the law of *karma*. Virtuous and vicious lifetimes lead to movements up or down the scale of classes in future lives. An evil-living *brahman* may fall to be a *sudra*, and vice versa. Such a system suggests a fair degree of flexibility and eschews any idea of purely hereditary characteristics. The fact that a person of, say, *brahman* qualities is born into a *brahman* family shows, not that the qualities were inherited from parents, but that the qualities won by worthy effort have 'earned' a place, time and circumstances suitable for their nurture. But does the flexibility extend to the 'earning' of superior class within one lifetime? Here the scriptures do not appear to be consistent. Often they state that the next lifetime brings with it the 'reward' or 'punishment' of a different class status. Yet occasionally they seem to allow for a more immediate transference of class.

> 'When a pious nature and pious deeds are noticeable in even a *Sudra*, he should be held superior to a person of the three regenerate classes. Neither birth, nor the purificatory rites, nor learning, nor offspring, can be regarded

as grounds for conferring upon one the regenerate status. Verily, conduct is the only ground.'

. . .

'If these characteristics be observable in a *Sudra*, and if they be not found in a *Brahmana*, then such a *Sudra* is no *Sudra*, and such a *Brahmana* is no *Brahmana*'
(*Mahabharata*, XI, p. 305; IX, p. 34)

A rather moving story in the *Chandogya* Upanishad illustrates this point. A young man wanted to study under a *brahman* sage. He asked his mother about his ancestry. She replied that he had been born when she was a servant girl, and she did not know his ancestry. Her name was Jabala and his was Satyakama. So she said he should call himself Satyakama Jabala. He went to the sage, who asked him of his lineage. The young man told him what his mother had said, and concluded, 'Sir, such as I am, I am Satyakama Jabala'. To which the sage replied 'A non-*brahman* would not be able to say this. I shall initiate you, since you did not depart from the truth.'

Thus class status is a consequence of former actions, rather than of hereditary traits. Birth clearly means birth as a person naturally endowed with certain qualities derived from earlier actions. This is confirmed by the sources that refer to the origin of class. *Brahman*, or *Krishna*, creates classes by assigning *gunas* and qualities. Indeed, were these to be hereditary, there would be no room for the divine creative power, except in the sense of the initial creation of a class system. For this reason, amongst others, there is no rational way in which class qualities can be assimilated to those of caste, for the latter are explicitly derived from mere status at birth, as the root of the word *jati* suggests.

Parallels in Western thought

The social system that Plato describes in his *Republic* and *Laws* is remarkably close to that of Vedanta with regard to classes. His guardians are devoted to the one good, indifferent to worldly attractions, learned in philosophy, own no property and serve the State from a sense of duty to the total exclusion of self-interest. Below them the auxiliaries are warriors, fierce in war, mild in peace, virtuous protectors of the State, who have recourse to the guardians for their education and spiritual welfare. The rest are traders, farmers, craftsmen and labourers, for whom Plato has little time, though he regards their well-being as equally dependent upon following a *métier* that matches their natural abilities. Justice in the State, as within the individual, rests upon harmony between its constituent orders or functions. Thus Plato, too, sees the natural distribution of qualities and actions to be the key to the health and prosperity of society. He also explicitly allows for the offspring of parents of a particular class to show themselves as destined for a higher or lower role.

Both in Plato and in later Western authorities, such as Alfred the Great, John of Salisbury and Edmund Burke, the idea of classes based upon natural qualities has been a powerful ingredient in political thought. However, its association with political conservatism rests upon the error of assuming that the distribution of qualities is correlated with hereditary factors. If, as Vedanta asserts, qualities are of divine origin but distributed according to previous actions, then it suggests that, on the contrary, a radical view of the social order is required. For if each person is to attain the status suitable to the qualities inherent in him, then a high degree of flexibility and social mobility is needed. An hereditary caste system is the antithesis of this.

Indeed history often reveals the degeneration of societies that initially exhibit a class structure based on natural qualities, and later degenerate into rigid caste systems. India itself is the outstanding example of this phenomenon. An interesting example in the West was France, where the *ancien régime* of the four classes of priests, aristocratic rulers, the third estate of lawyers, merchants and other professions, and the peasants became by the late 18th century a moribund caste system ripe for revolution. Not surprisingly, it was the frustrated talents of the third estate which gave impetus to the movement for reform, and finally for revolution. Earlier both Church and the administrative service had offered greater opportunities for talented 'inferiors' to rise in status.

Stages of life

Related to the four classes of Vedanta are the four stages of life: those of the student, the householder, the hermit and the mendicant. None of these are for the *sudra*, for he does not study the Veda, which is how the four stages begin. The three 'twice-born' classes, on the other hand, all have access to the stages of life, though probably the *vaisya* would rarely proceed beyond that of the householder. The student is guided by a teacher, or *guru*, ideally in the latter's home, and lives a life of celibacy and devotion to the service of his master. Law books, like *The Laws of Manu*, lay down strict rules for this service, such as deference in matters of eating, drinking, sitting down and retiring for the night. Besides the rigorous study of the Veda, mainly by means of recitation and memory, the student might also delve into the six related subjects (*vedangas*) of sacrifice, pronunciation, metre, etymology, grammar and astronomy.

After some years of study the young man becomes a householder. The 'triple aggregate' of virtue, wealth and pleasure is now enjoined. Marriage, trade or profession, and citizenship all have their place, though the class of the householder clearly influences the character of these. The duties of a householder remain closely prescribed. Diet and sleep are restrained; study and sacrifice continue – 'he should avoid malice and subdue his senses'. Treatment of relatives must be generous. This stage of life materially supports all the others in so far as only householders engage in economic activity. Hence it is incumbent upon them to support the other stages. The duty of hospitality to a guest, for example, is paramount. A wandering mendicant depends entirely upon it. One who turns away a guest loses all merit and takes upon himself the misdeeds of the shunned man. Finally, when the householder 'beholds the wrinkles on his body and white hair on his head and children of his children', he should himself adopt the life of a hermit.

Hermits take to the forest, abandoning family and possessions – though dutiful wives may accompany them. They strive for freedom from desires and the attractions of the world. They have no permanent home, though they may keep a cow and harvest wild grains. The elements of Sun, wind and rain offer them austerity. Meditation and prayer become the cornerstones of life.

In conclusion, the fourth stage of mendicancy is undertaken, characterized by renunciation. The mendicant wanders from place to place, dependent upon gifts. 'Withdrawn from every object, he should devote himself to his own self, taking pleasure in himself, and resting also on his own self.' (*Mahabharata*, IX, p. 194.) The *Gita* describes this final stage as that of a *sannyasin*, one who gives up or renounces.

> 'Unmoved in pleasure or in misery,
> Free from attachment to the world of sense,
> Equal in the face of praise and blame,
> Imbued with silence, ever satisfied,
> With no home but Myself.'
>
> (*Bhagavad Gita*, XII, 18–19, p. 102)

Even in ancient India, perhaps few men actually pursued all four stages of life in succession, though it remains an ideal for the most ardent and literal minded. Yet such a system, like that of the classes, is said to be divinely appointed. How then may the student of Vedanta practise such rules, especially in the circumstances of modern life? As elsewhere in Vedanta, the answer to this dilemma may be found by treating the four stages as models of the inner life for both men and women. Whatever the conditions, the seeker of truth may embark upon the serious study of the Veda, live a life of self-discipline (sexual restraint within marriage is equivalent to strict celibacy), follow the duties of the householder, and approach in due time the austerity of the hermit and the final renunciation of the mendicant, without actually taking to the forest or to the by-ways of mendicancy. The *Gita* does not define the *sannyasin* in terms of an outer life of beggary, but in terms of an inner life of sanctity. 'One that is a student', says the wise Vyasa in the *Mahabharata*, 'one that leads a life of domesticity, one that is a forest recluse, and one that leads a life of mendicancy, all reach the same high end by duly observing the duties of their respective modes of life.' (IX, p. 188.) Or as a modern Vedantist has put it, the four stages are steps to purification. The philosophy of Vedanta is not confined by houses or forests or begging bowls.

Afterword

Vedanta is not a philosophy on the lines of Western systems of thought, which can be fully expounded under such titles as empiricism, idealism or materialism. Still less can it be ascribed to individual thinkers or authors, as can the philosophies of Descartes or Berkeley, Hume or Kant, Hegel, Marx or (possibly) Wittgenstein. Therefore any book which claims to give an exhaustive account of Vedanta is necessarily misleading.

Thus an exposition of Vedanta is bound to be incomplete. For millennia, teachers and writers have contributed to it. None can be taken as the final authority, and even Sankara, widely regarded as the most authoritative source of *Advaita* Vedanta, undoubtedly would have denied that what he spoke or wrote was the final truth of Vedanta. The Upanishads themselves explicitly repudiate the idea that they state the truth. All that can be said with confidence of these teachers and writers, especially those in the tradition of *Advaita*, is that they point the way. They give direction to the aspirant who seeks the truth.

Yet paradoxically it would seem that Vedanta, more than other philosophies, rests upon one exceedingly simple proposition, namely that 'All is *Brahman*'. The problem is that to state this, or even to believe it, is insufficient. Knowledge of its truth is quite another thing, for Vedanta proposes that knowledge is not something that can be stated at all. Rather it is an aspect of *Brahman* itself and therefore absolute and beyond all human devices of speech, writing or thought. Such a view is not as strange as it may sound. Even on the level of mundane life, we would not regard our knowledge, say of a friend, to be equivalent to any mere statement or thought.

An exposition of Vedanta, nevertheless, may help to clarify why the one 'truth' that 'All is *Brahman*' is so central to it. Whichever area of Vedanta one enquires into leads back to this nodal point. As we have seen, if one examines the Vedantic explanation of the three states of waking, dreaming and sleeping, one is driven back to the question of to whom they belong. Who wakes, dreams and sleeps? Obviously the answer is oneself. But what is that? As Ramana Maharshi replied to a man who said that all he experienced in deep sleep was a blank, 'For whom is the blank?' Only by self-enquiry is the true study of Vedanta to be made; and that, we are assured by the Upanishads, concludes with the realization that the self is the one *Brahman*.

And if one looks into the Vedantic view of creation of the world, one finds that the 'world' is described as an unending superimposition upon the one reality. The whole account of the world as nature or *prakriti* – at least in *Advaita* – hinges upon the concept of *maya*, the dream of *Brahman*. Thus everything in time past, present and future is comprehended in *Brahman*, like the events in a film that are totally contained on the screen.

This absolute monism, or oneness, of *Advaita* Vedanta goes far to explain its open-ended form, which makes the task of explaining it as a system so tantalizing. For, as the master teachers always demonstrate, one can start anywhere and still be led back to the one central 'truth'. For this reason, some of the best presentations of Vedanta are in the form of simple stories or vivid analogies, rather than of philosophical treatises. No straight line account can do justice to it, for its profundities lie at every point in a limitless sphere, not at the end of a finite line. Of Vedanta it may verily be said that the end is the beginning. The search begins with oneself and ends with oneself. What matters is the direction.

Glossary of Sanskrit Terms

acharya: Spiritual guide or teacher.

Advaita: Non-dual; especially associated with *Advaita* Vedanta, which rejects the dualism of self and the world.

aham: 'I' or 'I am'.

ahankara: Ego; literally 'I am the doer'.

ajnana: Lack of knowledge; spiritual ignorance.

ananda: Pure happiness, bliss.

antakarana: 'the internal organ', or mind.

asat: Non-existence.

asi: You are [sing.] from Sanskrit verb '*as*'.

asmi: 'I am'; from Sanskrit verb '*as*'.

Atman: Individual self, which in reality is universal.

avidya: Ignorance or illusion.

ayam: This.

bhakti: Devotion or love.

Brahma: The creator god of the fundamental triad of deities.

Brahman: Universal self or spirit of the Universe.

brahmana: Member of the highest class, devoted to wisdom.

buddhi: Intelligence as a function of mind.

candala: Outcast; lowest of mixed classes.

chit: Knowledge or consciousness.

chitta: Heart or seat of emotions; memory, reflection.

dharma: Law, righteousness, justice, virtue.

dhatu: Seed form or stem of words.

dvaita: Dual, especially relating to self and world.

dvapara: Bronze age of 864,000 years.

gunas: Three constituent forces of the Universe.

guru: Respected person, especially a spiritual teacher.

hamsa: Swan, a symbol of the self.

Hiranyagarbha: Universal mind; literally 'golden foetus'.

jati: Caste as determined at birth.

jiva: Individual spirit or soul.

jnana: Knowledge of what really exists.

kali: Iron age of 432,000 years.

kalpa: One day of *Brahma*, or 1000 *mahayugas*.

kara: Doer, maker or author.

karma: Action; former act producing effect in a
      subsequent lifetime.

kartavya: Individual's inner awareness of 'what is to be done'.

krita: Golden age of 1,728,000 years.

kshatriya: Warrior or ruling class, including kings.

madhyama: Intermediate level of speech, where formulation
      begins.

mahayuga: Cycle of four ages totalling 4,320,000 years.

manas: Discursive function of mind.

manuvantara: One fourteenth of a day of *Brahma*, or seventy-
      one *mahayugas*.

maya: The world or nature seen as illusion, or the dream
      of Brahman.

nirguna: Beyond the *gunas*.

OM: The Word, representing *Brahman*, from which all
      creation emerges.

para: Furthest, ultimate; location associated with source of
      speech.

paribhuh: To be around or beyond.

pashyanti: 'Seeing'; the level of speech, where words are held
      in potential.

prakriti: Nature in both potential and manifest forms.

pranas: Five breaths which regulate the body.

puranas: Ancient tales or legends, supposedly written by Vyasa.

rajas: *Guna* of movement, activity and passion.

rishis: Wise men.

saguna: With, or attended by, the *gunas.*

samkalpa: Resolution or intention.

samsara: Experience of the world

samsarin: Experiencer of the world.

sandhi: Joining of letters to form modified sound; in general, the junction of times or events.

sannyasin: One who gives up or renounces; fourth and final stage of life.

sanskara: What individuals face as a consequence of former lives.

sat: Existence or being.

sattva: *Guna* of goodness, clarity and peace.

shabda: Word; *Shabda-Brahman* relates creation to *OM* as *Brahman.*

shaktis: Sixteen fundamental powers of *Brahman.*

Siva: The destroying god of the triad of deities.

smriti: Knowledge as recorded by enlightened scribes (literally 'remembered').

sphota: Explosion of consciousness, giving rise to meaning of words and sentences.

sruti: Revealed knowledge.

sudra: Member of the lowest class, suited for menial duties.

tamas: *Guna* of inertia and darkness.

tanmatras: Five subtle elements of earth, water, fire, air and space.

tattvam: 'That-thou'; used to refer to the identity of the world and the self.

treta: Silver age of 1,296,000 years.

upadhi: Limitations which the mind imposes upon the self.

vaikhari: 'Elaborated speech', utterance of vernacular language.

vaisya: Member of merchant, trading and farming class.

varna: Character or quality, especially of men as members of a
class (literally 'colour').

vayu: The element air or wind.

Veda: Ancient Sanskrit writings, derived from an oral tradition,
embodying knowledge said to be coeval with mankind.

vedanga: Six subjects of study connected to the *Veda*: sacrifice,
pronunciation, metre, etymology, grammar, astronomy.

Vedanta: Philosophical essence of the *Veda*; literally the end of
the *Veda*.

Viraj: Primeval man, as secondary creator after *Brahma*.

Vishnu: The sustaining or protecting god of the triad of deities.

yoga: Joining or union, especially practices to achieve union
with Brahman.

yugas: Four great successive ages in the cycles of time.

Bibliography

Books quoted, in order of appearance in text

John Donne, 'An Anatomie of the World: The First Anniversary' in *John Donne: Complete Poetry and Selected Prose*, Nonesuch, London, 1967

The Eight Upanishads (translation by Swami Gambhirananda), Advaita Ashrama, Calcutta, Vol .1, 1972, Vol. 2, 1978

Bhagavad Gita (translation by Brian Hodgkinson), Books for All, Delhi, 2003

The Ten Principal Upanishads (translation by Shree Purohit Swami and WB Yeats), Faber and Faber, London, 1938

T.S. Eliot, *Four Quartets*, Faber and Faber, London, 1970

Erwin Schrödinger, *'Nature and the Greeks' and 'Science and Humanism'*, Cambridge University Press, 1951

Brahma Sutra Bhasya (translation by Swami Gambhirananda), Advaita Ashrama, Calcutta, 1977

Chandogya Upanishad (translation by Swami Gambhirananda), Advaita Ashrama, Calcutta, 2003

The Crest Jewel of Wisdom (translation by Charles Johnston), John M. Watkins, London, 1964

David Hume, *A Treatise of Human Nature*, Everyman, London, 1956

Brihadaranyaka Upanishad (translation by Swami

Madhavananda), Advaita Ashrama, Calcutta, 1965

Talks with Sri Ramana Maharshi, V.S. Ramanan, Sri
   Ramanasramam, Tiruvannamalai, 2000

Samkara on the Absolute, Vol. 1, from *Samkara Source Book*,
   (translation by AJ Alston), Shanti Sadan, London, 2005

N. Malcolm, *Ludwig Wittgenstein: A Memoir*, Oxford University
   Press, 1958

William Shakespeare, *Macbeth*

Plato, *Timaeus*, in *The Dialogues of Plato*, (translation by B.
   Jowett), 2 vols, Random House, New York, 1937

Vakyavritti of Sri Sankaracharya, (translation by Swami
   Jagadananda), Sri Ramakrishna Math, Mylapore, 1973

M. Gladwell, *Blink*, Allen Lane, London, 2005

Ludwig Wittgenstein, *Philosophical Investigations*, (translation by
   G.E.M. Anscombe), Blackwell, Oxford, 2001

The Orange Book, The Society for the Study of Normal
   Psychology, London, 1981

Shantanand Saraswati, *Birth and Death*, The Study Society,
   London, 1993

Thomas Traherne, *Centuries*, The Faith Press, London, 1963

AL Basham, *The Wonder that was India*, Sidgwick and Jackson,
   London, 1982

S. Radhakrishnan, *Indian Philosophy*, Oxford University Press,
   2002

Adhyatma Ramayana (translation by Swami Tapasyananda),
   Sri Ramakrishna Math, Madras, 1985

William Shakespeare, *The Sonnets*

Mahabharata (translation by K.S. Ganguli), 2 vols, Munshiram
   Manoharlat, New Delhi, 1976

The Laws of Manu (translation by G. Bühler), Motilal
   Banarsidass, Delhi, 1982

Srimad Bhagavatam (translation by Swami Prabhavananda),
   Sri Ramakrishna Math, Madras, 1972

Plato, *The Republic*, in *The Dialogues of Plato* (translation by B.
   Jowett), 2 vols, Random House, New York, 1937

T. Nagel, *What Does It All Mean?*, Oxford University Press, New York, 1987

B.N.K. Sharma, *The Brahmasutras and their Principal Commentaries*, Munshiram Manoharlal, Bombay, 1986

Other books

Ashtadhyayi of Panini (translation by Srisra Chandra Vasu), 2 vols, Motilal, Delhi, 1977

Ashtavakra Gita (translation by Hari Prasad Shastri), Shanti Sadan, London, 1972

George Berkeley, *The Principles of Human Knowledge*, Collins, London, 1977

Bhagavad Gita, with Sankara commentary (translation by Alladi Mahadeva Sastry), Samata, Madras, 1977

P. Deussen, *Outline of the Vedanta System of Philosophy According to Sankara* (translation by J.H. Woods and C.B. Runkle), Cambridge University Press, 1915

A. Farndell, *A Mahabharata Companion*, St James, London, 2003

P.M.S. Hacker, *Wittgenstein's Place in Twentieth-Century Analytic Philosophy*, Blackwell, Oxford, 1997

Hesiod, *Theogony, Works and Days* (translation by M.L. West), Oxford University Press, 1988

Immanuel Kant, *Critique of Pure Reason* (translation by W.S. Pluhar), Hacket, Indianapolis, 1996

— *The Moral Law* (translation by H.J. Paton), Hutchinson, London, 1961

Mahatma Dattatreya, *Avadhut Gita*, (translation by Hari Prasad Shastri), Shanta Sadan, London, 1968

M. Müller, *The Six Systems of Indian Philosophy*, London, 1899

Ramayana of Valmiki, (translation by Hari Prasad Shastri), 3 vols, Shanti Sadan, London, 1962

G. Ryle, *Concept of Mind*, Hutchinson, London, 1975

Sankara, *The Nectar-Ocean of Enlightenment*, (translation by Samvid), Samata, Madras, 1993

Shantanand Saraswati, *Good Company*, Element, Shaftesbury,
  1987

— *The Man who wanted to meet God*, Element, Shaftesbury, 1996

Arvind Sharma, *Classical Hindu Thought*, Oxford University Press,
  2000

Swami Nikhilananda, *Self-Knowledge*, Sri Ramakrishna Math,
  Madras, 1947

Varadaraja, *Laghukaumudi* (Sanskrit grammar) (translation by JR
  Ballantyne), Motilal, Delhi, 1976

Index